What Your Autistic Child Wants You to Know

of related interest

The Asperkid's (Secret) Book of Social Rules, 10th Anniversary Edition
Jennifer Cook
ISBN 978 1 78775 837 7
eISBN 978 1 78775 838 4

The Spectrum Girl's Survival Guide
How to Grow Up Awesome and Autistic
Siena Castellon
Foreword by Temple Grandin
ISBN 978 1 78775 183 5
eISBN 978 1 78775 184 2

Simple Autism Strategies for Home and School
Practical Tips, Resources and Poetry
Sarah Cobbe
Foreword by Glenys Jones
ISBN 978 1 78592 444 6
eISBN 978 1 78450 817 3

The Little Book of Autism FAQs
How to Talk with Your Child about their Diagnosis and Other Conversations
Davida Hartman
Illustrated by Margaret Anne Suggs
ISBN 978 1 78592 449 1
eISBN 978 1 78450 824 1

The Complete Guide to Asperger's Syndrome
Tony Attwood
ISBN 978 1 84985 789 5
eISBN 978 1 84642 559 2

WHAT YOUR AUTISTIC CHILD WANTS YOU TO KNOW

And How You Can Help Them

Maja Toudal

Foreword by Tony Attwood

Illustrated by Signe Sønderhousen

Jessica Kingsley Publishers

London and Philadelphia

First published in Great Britain in 2022 by Jessica Kingsley Publishers
An imprint of Hodder & Stoughton Ltd
An Hachette Company

1

Front cover image source: Adobe Stock.

A CIP catalogue record for this title is available from the
British Library and the Library of Congress

ISBN 978 1 78775 772 1
eISBN 978 1 78775 773 8

Printed and bound in the United States by
Integrated Books International

Jessica Kingsley Publishers' policy is to use papers that are natural, renewable and recyclable products and made from wood grown in sustainable forests. The logging and manufacturing processes are expected to conform to the environmental regulations of the country of origin.

Jessica Kingsley Publishers
Carmelite House
50 Victoria Embankment
London EC4Y 0DZ

www.jkp.com

To my family, who try their best to understand even when it is difficult, and who listen when I try to explain.

Contents

Foreword

Young children who have autism have great difficulty describing their thoughts, feelings and experiences. They have a different way of perceiving, thinking, learning and relating, and family members and teachers need to know how to accommodate those differences. Eventually, the child may be able to articulate what others need to know. However, that knowledge is already available from mature autistic adults, such as Maja Toudal.

Maja is able to conceptualize and clearly explain the many aspects of autism, based on her own experiences and on conversations with some of the leading specialists in autism spectrum disorders. She knows what parents need to know.

Autism affects so many aspects of life, hence the wide range of topics covered in this comprehensive book, from making friends to pocket money. Maja also includes quotations from other autistic adults and adolescents and provides her own wise advice.

Over a number of years, Maja and I have enjoyed many conversations regarding the nature of autism, and I have absorbed and now incorporate many of her recommendations in my own clinical practice.

This book will become a valued resource at home and in the classroom.

Tony Attwood, Minds & Hearts Clinic, Brisbane, Australia

Acknowledgments

There are so many people without whom this book would never have happened, and I want to thank them here.

First and foremost, I want to thank the many amazing autistic people who shared their thoughts and experiences with me and allowed me to pass on their words through this book. Whether anonymous or named, their perspective is vital, and will certainly resonate with many.

Thank you to the autistic beta-readers who took the time to give me their perspective on the first drafts. The changes you inspired made this a better book, and I hope will be helpful to so many parents and carers.

I must also express my sincerest gratitude to Dr. Tony Attwood, who gave me the inspiration to begin writing this book and provided detailed comments, endless guidance and immeasurable moral support.

Signe Sønderhousen (Yondoloki), for her beautiful cover and illustrations which bring life and inspiration to the messages I hope to convey.

Anne Skov Jensen, for helping me so much when I felt that time was running out and I didn't know what to do or where to turn.

Sanne and Frederik, for donating their time and skills to help me make a point visual and for making it look cool.

Kirsten Callesen, for giving me the confidence to speak my mind.

Pia, for so many painstakingly long hours correcting my grammar.

Christian and Line for the long conversations, their guidance and invaluable professional input.

Gerd, for taking the time to provide comments and helping me to see this book from an outside perspective.

Even though my first language is Danish, and my English may be imperfect, I have chosen to write and publish this book in English to make sure that my words, and the words of my fellow autistic people who have contributed to this book, can reach a greater audience.

I want the reader to know that almost everyone involved in this project is autistic. Autistic people contributed, beta-read, illustrated and did the first round of editing. Some of the contributors are Danes, like me, and I want to let their words stand as they are because this is their book, as much as it is mine.

These are our words to our parents and to parents of children who are like us.

Introduction

There are so many things I wish I could have told my parents when I was a child, but back then I did not have the words. I could not explain. This, in itself, is one of the important things to know about children with autism spectrum disorders (ASD). There is so much going on behind the scenes, but for us, it can be very difficult to hold a thought and express it in words. As I became a teenager and young adult, I saw the benefit in learning to communicate through words. For this project, I have allied myself with autistic adults, young adults and teenagers, as well as specialized professionals, to provide comprehensive and personal insight into our perspective.

In ASD, there are key elements that you must understand to help autistic people. Some professionals may give you one set of rules to remember which revolve around recognizing our areas of difficulties. The "rules" I am going to list are different in some ways.

WE ARE HUMAN BEINGS, NO MATTER HOW DIFFERENT WE SEEM.

No matter how the autism is expressed and how complex the support needs, no matter how many sensory issues, social impairments, difficulties in executive functions or differences in perception, we are human. This does not make us any less different, but it also means we are very similar in so many ways. Unfortunately, many people can view us as inferior or defective, and we need you to show us that we are not. We need you to show us that we are equal, with both our differences and similarities.

Non-speaking autistic people are often perceived as intellectually impaired, and they often are treated as such. This is unfortunate, because whether someone speaks or not does not determine their intellect.

No matter who your child is, you should always assume that any treatment of them as intellectually impaired or disabled will be perceived by them, and that it will affect their self-worth. This does not mean that they should not be given help or support, just that it should be given with respect.

Another point to make here is that it is vital that you get rid of any preconceived notion that autism is something that is "wrong" with your child. We are different, not wrong. Hopefully by the time you have read this book, you will see what I mean when I say that even though autism can make life very challenging, it should not be viewed as something bad, but rather, an intrinsic part of your child.

THERE IS SOMETHING IN THIS WORLD THAT WE ARE GREAT AT.

Sometimes there are so many difficulties in our lives that we, and everyone around us, forget this. But there is something out there that each of us is great at, and not only do we need to find it, we also need the confidence to try it out. And much harder than that, sometimes we also need the conviction and perseverance to keep working on it or to keep doing it, when either we or people around us tell us we are no good. But when we find this ability, whatever it is, and we find out that we are good at it, it becomes a great joy. Perhaps even more so, because we are always (made) so aware of all the abilities we do not have.

WE ARE DIFFERENT FROM EVERY OTHER AUTISTIC PERSON.

I should not have to say this, but many people still assume that each autistic person will have many of the same traits, same interests, same style of communication and so on.

We each have our own personality. This has an effect on how our autism is expressed. We also have different profiles, different expressions and different experiences. Add to this also that each person will have different levels and types of sensory sensitivity. We are all different, just like non-autistic people are all different.

Each autistic person is as different (and as similar) to the next autistic person as each non-autistic person is.

WE NEED LOVE.

We may not need it expressed in the same way that you do, but we do still need it. If your child does not like to be touched or hugged, you may perceive that as a rejection. However, your child may express and want to receive love in other ways. (You may also have a child who loves hugs. Many autistic people do.)

Our expression of love can be the smallest things, which you might not connect with the notion of interpersonal love or affection. It can be putting our school bag in our room or placing it off of the floor because you have expressed a preference for that. It can be giving you a toy to cheer you up when you are sad, because we know that getting one would make us feel better. It can even be that we make an effort to stay at the dinner table for five minutes longer, because we know that you will prefer it.

No matter what, we need to be loved just as you do. I will suggest that one of the greatest sources for this may be a pet. This is not to diminish the love that you have for your child, but rather an understanding of how overwhelming human expressions of love can be for your child. Animals are easier to understand, and their expressions of emotions are much less complicated. Because of this, it may be that a person with ASD may feel more relaxed when there are animals around. Because animals can relax us, because they can feel simpler to understand and be around, they can be a wonderful way for us to enjoy companionship, even when human interaction is overwhelming.

They will never replace your love as a parent. However, they may be helpful in our learning about what expressions of love we are comfortable with giving and receiving, and this can be invaluable.

WE NEED SPACE.

Especially from people. Again, this is because humans are so overwhelming to be around, and the only restorative, aside from our special interest(s), is solitude. This is not a rejection of you personally, it is a need for restorative time which we cannot access in any other way.

Always remember that there is a big difference between being alone and being lonely. The two are not synonymous for autistic people. We can be lonely, but for the most part, being alone is something positive. Please allow us to have this.

WE ARE TRYING.

Sometimes the people around us get frustrated with all the things we cannot do. Sometimes, they (you) might even think we are just lazy, or not putting enough effort into learning the skills or coping mechanisms we should learn.

I am here to tell you that most autistic people would love to be able to just do all the things we are supposed to, and all the things normal people can do. When autism hinders us in our lives, we wish it did not, as much as anyone around us. We are constantly trying to learn, trying to cope. We just do not always have the capacity to show what is going on, or to truly know what we are even trying to achieve. We just try. We need help, and we are trying.

SOMETIMES WE NEED A DAY OFF.

And yes, there are days when we just do not want to, just as you have days when the prospect of going to work sucks, or you had days in school when you felt like having a day off from homework.

Well, imagine never having had a day off in your life. Imagine the prospect of never having a day off for the rest of your life, either. Imagine that the only time you can ever relax is when you are alone. We need to know that we will have time alone soon, preferably scheduled. I realize that saying this to any parent who has children seems like an insult. Saying this to a parent of a child who has an ASD diagnosis might seem like a slap in the face.

I truly hope, by the time you have read this book, you will understand what I mean when I phrase it the way I do, and that you will understand that it is not meant to diminish everything you do as a parent.

I trust that you will already know that, sometimes, everyone needs to take the pressure off. We do, too.

OUR ENERGY IS SPENT QUICKER.

This seems silly to say, and may seem like an insult to others, but I have come to realize that when it comes to anything other than special interest(s), my perceived energy storage, regeneration and capacity are just not the same as they are for someone who is not autistic. Or perhaps it is not that the capacity is smaller, but that there are so many more things that we have to process all the time. Whatever the reason, I seem to be more prone to fatigue and exhaustion, and I hear the same from my autistic peers.

Try to picture it as a laptop computer or a tablet. When you are running on batteries, you will be able to see quite clearly, that if you have 10 programs (apps) running, the batteries will drain quicker than if you were only running two programs. Now, any person is much the same. If all your sensory and social processing are separate programs that you have to actively open and run and work in, this will drain you more quickly than if they are automatic programs running in the background.

WE NEED YOU TO CATCH US, NOT CARRY US.

There is a term in Denmark for parents who sweep away the problems their children might face before they even appear. These are called "curling-parents." This is from the sport curling, in which the ice is swept in front of the stone, to allow it to travel further and stay straight on its path. This is what not to do. Of course, we need support though. Everyone needs to know that someone will catch them if they fall; but being there, with your arms stretched out ready to catch, does not mean holding us down when we try to jump, or lifting us up so we can reach without trying.

In cheerleading, there are people responsible for catching the flyer (the person doing stunts in the air). Of course, they're also responsible for throwing her into in air in the first place, but for the sake of this analogy, we will ignore that part. No flyer would want to go that high up and do all those dangerous and impressive stunts without knowing they will arrive safely on the ground. That is your job. You are there to catch us so we do not get hurt too badly. Never mind a bruise or two, we learn from those; just prevent torn ligaments and broken bones, okay? Probably the most important component in catching rather than carrying is that you should believe in your child. Believe that they will be okay, that they will learn what they need to, in their own time.

There are many parents who look at famous autistic people and say things like: "But that is him/her... my child's autism is much more severe. They will never be able to do that."

The thing is, what you see when you look at those famous individuals is the end result of many years of hard work, of learning skills and strategies/coping mechanisms and applying them. These people have often spent many years developing workaround strategies that are still being actively used in their everyday life, and you are likely not seeing or hearing about these. You are not seeing the difficult childhood years when social efforts failed miserably, when they were plagued by feelings of inferiority and even suicidal thoughts. You see the person that came through those struggles. But when you see your child, right now, you are seeing the hard years. It can be hard to combine the two images and see the possibility that your child can learn amazing skills and can become very successful in life. The fact is it is possible, and your child needs to believe in this: that they can have a successful and happy future. Because if you do not see it, why and how should they?

WE WANT YOU TO CHILL.

I know it is hard. It is much easier said than done. There are many challenges involved in having an autistic child, and this is possibly the hardest.

But there is a reason. Your child picks up on your stress, anger and anxiety. All children do this, but we are very sensitive to it because we have no filter. When you are stressed and anxious, we become stressed and anxious, too—we just do not know why. Then we function worse, which gives you another reason (no matter what the initial one was) to be stressed and anxious, and then the downward spiral has begun.

If you are calm, if you have hope that everything will be okay, then that is "contagious," too. If you believe in us, we are given confidence and strength to keep going in life. And the importance of this cannot be understated.

Lastly, I want you to know that I understand that no parent will ever be perfect. If you took every piece of advice given, taking into account your child's profile and personality, you will still do something wrong. Asking you to do everything I talk about in this book would be asking a human to be superhuman. It cannot be done.

This book is not a guide that should be followed to the letter. I recognize that not every child will present in the same way, and that the advice here tends towards the experience of autistic children and young people who are verbal. However, I also hope that the insights are universal enough that by reading them you will feel a little closer to the autistic experience generally and have a better understanding of how any autistic child might view the world.

The book is divided into two parts: Part 1 provides some background knowledge about autism, and Part 2 looks at some specific aspects of childhood and growing up. These sections are meant to be read in a "dip-in, dip-out" way, so you can jump straight to the information that feels most relevant. All the material is connected, but some specific suggestions for related content are included at the start of each Part 2 chapter.

This is not a prescriptive book designed to be read from start to finish; rather, it is an attempt at providing you with the inside perspective, so you understand not only what your child might need, but why. It is an attempt at translating and offering advice.

> Trigger warning: Please note that throughout the book, and particularly in the chapters "Bullying and Peer Pressure" and "Harmful Strategies and Risky Behavior," complex subjects such as self-harm and suicide are discussed. Please scan the headings before reading if you wish to avoid certain topics.

◇ Part I ◇

EXPLAINING THE BASICS

In Part 1, we look at how autism is defined and diagnosed, and how having an autistic child can affect you and your wider family. We also introduce the ASD way of thinking and perceiving and consider some of the key issues from an autistic point of view.

◇ Section 1 ◇

Getting Started

You

The very first topic I want to address is your side of the family dynamic. I am very aware that much of my advice requires that the rest of the family takes the autistic child's needs into account first and leaves their own needs aside for later. No one should reasonably expect you to do this at all times and with all things. That is not what this book is for.

I have heard so many mothers, fathers and siblings expressing worries that they are not doing enough or that what they are doing is wrong or inadequate, and I will tell you the same thing I have told every single one of them: You cannot take care of your child if you have not taken care of yourself. You need to be okay with you. You need to find, first and foremost, a way to relieve your stress, to relax, to get the sleep you need and have something good to eat. You need to schedule time for your own hobby, a night to read quietly or a cheerful lunch with a friend.

If you neglect yourself, you will have nothing left to give. Your child needs you to be okay, too.

And the rest of the family needs to be okay. They need time to do the things they love or find relaxing because otherwise you will end up with a problem in your family dynamics—a culture in which the person with ASD makes the rules and sets the schedule for everyone—and ultimately this is not beneficial to anyone.

Because it can cause issues when the needs of the rest of the family are neglected in favour of the needs of the autistic person, I want to emphasize, very specifically, the point that the suggestions and advice in this book are meant as just that—suggestions and advice, and there is no expectation that all of them will be implemented. You need to find the compromises that work in your family, for all the people in your family.

You, your spouse and any additional children are every bit as important members of the family as the autistic child, and none of you should be expected to give up everything in an effort to meet impossible standards, such as would be set by this book if one attempted to do everything. Please, take care of you, too.

Additionally, I know that many parents of autistic children will be used to parents of non-autistic children giving them all sorts of advice or blaming them for their child's autism, their challenges, and so on. Because of this, I do want to make it clear that it is okay for you to not take that advice, you do not deserve the blame that is thrown at you, and you do not need to apologize for not being gracious about the things people say to you. You are trying your best, and that is all anyone can do.

Autism

In 2013, the *Diagnostic and Statistical Manual of Mental Disorders* (DSM), one of the main resources setting out the definition of autism for clinicians, was updated with the issue of the 5th edition (American Psychiatric Association 2013). In this edition, autism, infantile autism, Asperger's syndrome and several other diagnoses were all lumped into the new diagnosis: autism spectrum disorder. In this, there are three specified "levels" of ASD, of which 1 is the "mildest" and 3 is the most "severe."

This is not really news at all, since professionals recognized the previous diagnoses as being related under the term autism spectrum disorder (or autism spectrum condition, which is a term many of those with the diagnoses prefer as it pathologizes us slightly less). However, the new criteria do make it harder for some to get a clinical diagnosis where previously they would have gotten one.

The DSM is written by the American Psychiatric Association, and some countries still use completely different diagnostic manuals, so depending on which country you live in, Asperger's, infantile autism and so on, may still be current diagnoses. This means that in the global community, there is now some confusion as to whether or not Asperger's and other diagnoses are still "real" diagnoses or not. There are many who have received these diagnoses in the past, and many more will in the countries that do not use the DSM to diagnose people. And as we already knew that Asperger's, for example, was a part of the autistic spectrum, I do not see the diagnoses as separate at all. Basically, Asperger's syndrome has simply changed its name to ASD-1.

In this book there will be references to Asperger's along with autism, in part because some of the people who have contributed with their own perspectives have the diagnosis Asperger's syndrome, rather than ASD. This means only that their diagnosis was given prior to the changes, or that they are from a country where another diagnostic system is used. There is a lot of research regarding Asperger's syndrome which is still valid, and there is a significant amount of literature out there on the topic.

While the diagnoses are not the same—there are differences in the diagnostic criteria—many professionals do not see the need to keep these diagnoses separate and neither do autistic people themselves. We are all a part of the same community and while our support needs vary greatly (even within the same diagnoses as they existed in DSM-IV or as they do in other systems), we share many of the same perspectives and experiences. As such, any distinctions made between diagnoses in this book should be seen in this light.

◇ Section 2 ◇

A–Z of Key Issues

Amygdala and Emotions

The amygdala is a part of the brain which is involved with recognizing, processing and regulating emotions. Studies have shown differences in the amygdala of autistic people and non-autistic people. The difference we have means that, comparatively, we have difficulties with regulating our emotions, consciously perceiving and processing the emotions of ourselves and others, and regulating our reactions to these emotions. The explanation here is simplified, as it is intended for people who do not have, or need, extensive knowledge on neurobiology or neuropsychology. For those who know these things, I hope they forgive the simplification, and for those who need additional knowledge, I recommend looking for recent academic literature—any specific recommendations I could offer would be likely outdated in a short period of time.

It is not universal, of course, but autistic people tend to feel in neutrals and extremes. If we picture the range of an emotion of a scale of 0–10, 0 being neutral, then the average person will spend very little time in the 8–10 range of any emotion. Those levels are triggered only by traumatic or otherwise big events, such as being cheated on, losing a steady income (having their livelihood threatened) or a death in the family, and on the scale of happiness it might be getting a hard-earned promotion, being proposed to, becoming a parent, and so on.

Autistic people can feel great levels of frustration or despair if we are five minutes late for school or left our pencil-case at home. Likewise, we can feel extreme happiness at getting a perfect score on a spelling test or finding an extra item for our collection (which is a special interest of many of us).

We can also have a surprisingly neutral reaction to some things. Importantly, the things we do or do not react to depend on the person: what is and is not important to them currently. The result is that while the average person spends most time in the 0–5 range, and it takes a lot for them to go above 7, autistic people spend most time between 0–3 and 8–10. It is quite possible to be in-between, as it is possible for someone non-autistic (in this book, people who are not autistic are also referred to as allistic) to be at 8–10, but this is an indicator of how our emotional life generally is.

The trouble with this is that, especially as children, autistic people will have a tendency to skip everything between 2 or 3 and 8. If we forget our pencil-case, as mentioned in the earlier example, we go to school feeling fairly content, say happy at a 1—a somewhat neutral emotional state, but positive—then the moment we realize that our pencil-case is not in our school bag, we may very well go straight from happy 1, to despair 9.

> Life tends to be either "happy" or "not happy," "angry" or "not angry." All the "in between" emotions on the continuum get missed. I jump from calm to panic in one major step. (Lawson 2001, p.119)

This is quite frustrating for the autistic person, as well as for those around us. As you can probably imagine, being at negative emotional extremes is not pleasant, and once we develop the ability to realize that others do not respond well to these emotional outbursts it will make us embarrassed, and we will often become afraid of being in situations that may cause extreme emotions because we want to avoid the shame and embarrassment. This tendency for our emotional life to be experienced in extremes will influence much of the advice in this book.

Cognitive Abilities

This term refers to, among other things, thinking and learning abilities. When we talk about cognitive abilities, we are talking about how you process the world around you. I will give a few examples. One cognitive ability is verbal comprehension or verbal reasoning. This is not only about whether or not you know the words, but also how flexibly you can process and use them. It also has to do with the ability to understand, explain and use abstract words and concepts, such as "love." Another cognitive ability is working memory, which refers to how much new information you can keep in your mind while working with it. Processing speed is another, which has to do with how quickly you are able to work with the information. There are more; however, I shall leave the explanation as is, as this is not intended to be a full crash-course on the topic but merely an introduction.

In non-autistic people, conventional knowledge says that these abilities are usually quite balanced. But this is not necessarily the case in autistic people. Our cognitive ability profile can be extremely unbalanced. This phrasing may sound quite strange. In effect, think of each type of cognitive ability being measured on a scale and these scales being arranged side by side for comparison. In non-autistic people, the scales will often be quite close to one another in their measures, meaning that if you were to draw a line across the measures, it would be somewhat straight. In autistic people, that line can be very uneven. This means that an autistic person who may be able to teach themselves to read, spell and solve mathematical problems, can at the same time not have the ability to find their way around a school, for example.

There is a tendency to have a one-track mind and to be unable to steer off a particular course of thinking, even after we have realized it is not a helpful strategy. Usually there is also a great fear of making mistakes. On top of this, there is a tendency toward attention problems at school—many of which have to do with our focus on detail and inability to control this—as well as problems in executive functioning. This includes organization and planning, working memory, impulse control, time management, prioritizing, understanding abstract concepts, and so on. Think of it as the CEO in our brains being a scatter-brained and disorganized person, and you have the general idea. An autistic girl described one way in which her problems in executive functioning reveal themselves:

> "It's easy doing things when I'm already doing them, but what is difficult is getting started and finishing tasks. I find it extremely frustrating and I've spoken to many psychologists and other professionals about it, trying to find solutions." (Anonymous, personal communication)

There are many fancy words that cover our problems and discrepancies in our cognitive abilities, but what I mostly need you to take away from this is that your child's ability to think and learn in different situations and their different academic and life skills will possibly be very unbalanced/uneven. And you may become very frustrated at times, thinking: "Why can they not do this, when they are so smart!?" I want you to know that whatever we are good and not so good at are probably not connected, and you should expect very different learning curves.

Your child might be able to read and understand books that are several grades ahead, but not be able to put their t-shirt on the right way. Likewise, they may be able to draw or paint the most incredible and photorealistic art, but not be able to grasp the difference between five minutes and an hour.

As one of the most famous people with autism, Temple Grandin, describes in one of her books:

> My mind is completely visual and spatial work such as drawing is easy. I taught myself drafting in six months. I have designed big steel and concrete cattle facilities, but remembering a phone

> number or adding up numbers in my head is still difficult. I have to write them down. Every piece of information I have memorized is visual. (Grandin 1984, p.145)

Our thinking and learning abilities are very unpredictable, and may also change very suddenly, especially due to maturity, hormonal changes and/or traumatic events.

You will be frustrated, and you will probably never completely understand why they can do one thing but not another. That is okay. We also feel frustrated about this, perhaps even more so at times. However, it is a part of being an autistic person.

One autistic man wrote to me about this:

> "I'm still incapable of skateboarding, as in standing on and moving forwards, or even diving into a swimming pool. Trampolines are deathtraps. And basketball would likely still present challenges, just with having to dribble the ball once every two steps. It's frustrating as an adult, but infuriating as a child. One can easily begin to feel defective." (Scott, personal communication)

Because it can make us feel defective, or wrong, and because it is so difficult emotionally that we may not be able to do "normal" things, you may have to put in extra work to support us in noticing our talents and skills.

Co-Morbidity

This term refers simply to one or more additional diagnoses co-occurring with the primary one. There are many different diagnoses one might have, while also being autistic. Some of the most common ones are ADHD (Attention Deficit Hyperactivity Disorder), anxiety, depression and OCD (Obsessive Compulsive Disorder).

It is always a challenge as an autistic person to live in a society which is not made for people like us, but additional diagnoses can add greatly to this challenge.

It is important to remember that being autistic changes the way you perceive the world, and autism will also affect the way any additional diagnosis is expressed and the way it should be treated. Therefore, it is important to make sure that the people involved in treating your child have specialized education in autism.

It is also very important to understand where one diagnosis ends and the other begins, and how they overlap. Your job in educating yourself not only doubles with each additional diagnosis, but ever so slightly more.

The most important part is, of course, to make sure that you are not learning the theory of how the diagnoses *should* interact, but instead how they actually *do* interact in your child. Your child's autistic profile has a great deal to say about how they might be affected by, for example, anxiety. How severe the anxiety is adds yet another dynamic to consider. How it will affect the dynamic differs from person to person. The professional who diagnosed or works with your child will likely be able to help you uncover and understand the specific ways in which this applies to your child. Your child also needs to learn these things as they grow up and get older, as having a greater understanding of their profile and diagnoses will increase their ability to create a happy and fulfilling life for themselves.

It is very difficult to know yourself well enough to know which of your diagnoses or difficulties happens to be the primary one affecting you right now, so it will be even more difficult for you to know it for your child. It is not easy for them to learn, yet if they can, it will help them significantly. So, it is a good place to put in some extra effort.

Empathy and Sympathy

First, I will have to define these words to make sure my meaning comes through correctly. So here are the definitions I am working with:

> Empathy: the ability to share (resonate with) and understand the feelings of another.
>
> Sympathy: feelings of compassion and sorrow for someone else's misfortune.

There are then two parts to having empathy: one is to share an emotion; the other is to understand an emotion. Having sympathy is a seemingly simpler matter, in that the concept deals with whether you feel compassion or not. These terms are simplified here, in order to explain briefly rather than going into a lot of detail.

It is said by some that autistic people do not have empathy. This is not true. Some of us can have difficulties picking up on what others are feeling. Many of us do pick up on and resonate with these emotions. The problem is not always that we do not know if you are in pain, but rather that we cannot cope with the emotion—it is too big and it hurts—and also because we do not necessarily know where the emotion comes from. We do not know the *why*. So, we could say that we both do and do not have empathy.

However, this does not mean that we are awful people who do not care. Because while we may not know why you are in pain, and we are afraid of doing the wrong thing when trying to "fix it," we certainly do not want you to be in pain. If we are to state it very shortly and very simply, we can have difficulties in empathy, or certain parts of it, but we do have sympathy.

In Tony Attwood's (2007) book, *The Complete Guide to Asperger's Syndrome*, he discusses a quote from Nita Jackson in which she describes making one of the types of mistakes which might make it seem that we lack sympathy:

> I discovered that I couldn't comprehend people's facial expressions, what they said or the way in which they said it. Reminiscing on my early school days I realized how I used to laugh when someone cried because I thought the other person was laughing. I can't understand how I made this mistake – all I know is that I did this often. (Jackson 2002, p.20)

Considering this example, Dr. Attwood notes that: "The extreme facial expressions for someone crying and laughing can be very similar. Both emotions can produce tears. The confusion for someone with Asperger's syndrome is quite understandable but can be misinterpreted by others" (Attwood 2007, p.153).

So, a misunderstanding occurs twice in such a situation. First, we misread crying as laughing, which makes us laugh "with" this other person. The person who is crying and other onlookers then assume that we know that the person is, in fact, crying, not laughing, and so they will judge our laughter as cruelty. Such situations do not happen for all autistic people, but for some it can be a challenge in everyday life.

Whenever you see your child (or someone else you know is autistic) not giving the correct response to an emotion, it is important to remember they are most likely not cold and uncaring; rather they have probably either shut down because the emotion is too overwhelming for them to cope with, or they do not know the correct way to respond, and perhaps they either misinterpreted the situation or chose to do nothing out of fear of making a mistake.

The different ways we experience emotions (see Amygdala and Emotions) can mean we have some issues with empathy, in that it can be hard for us to relate to emotions that we have never felt. (It should be noted that this is true for everyone, though that is a whole different topic.)

If we put emotions on a scale from 0–10, where 0 is neutral and 10 is extreme, we can explore this in relatively simple terms. If you are angry at level 6, but I have only ever experienced anger at 1–2 or 9–10, then I do not know what 6 feels like.

When I get older and I learn to recognize the in-between emotions, I may suddenly relate emotionally to events that happened many years ago, but as a child it is very difficult. Keep this in mind when discussing emotions with your child.

A good tool to use for communication regarding emotions and the scale of them, is the CAT-Kit, developed by Kirsten Callesen and Tony Attwood. You can find this online at www.cat-kit.com.

How to Give Advice

The first thing to note is that there is no way to guarantee the desired result. I cannot promise you that anything I write here will be spot on.

Encourage asking for help to solve problems. This is the best thing in the long term, because once we learn that it is okay to ask for help, and getting help does not mean we are stupid, then we will be more receptive to help and advice in general.

Be careful of criticism. Make it either neutral or positive. Be like a GPS: keep emotions out and focus on the task. If you go a different way than the GPS suggests it will not yell or get angry, and it will not criticize your driving skills; it will simply calculate a new route and tell you the new instructions.

Stay away from "You are not doing it right" and "Can't you see...?" and try adapting your language into "I think others have maybe had the same problem. Maybe someone has already found a solution. We can try searching online?" Of course, when dealing with homework, searching online for answers might not be the way to go. Be careful of "butting in" and forcing help and advice on your child. If they are still in the "I can figure it out myself!" mode, then they are not likely to be happy to accept advice. This can be very hard, I know. However, it can help the process of teaching your child to ask for help, because they will not have the experience that help is something others force on you, but something you choose to ask for when you need it.

Offer knowledge, but do not act superior. To explain this properly, I will include a widely shared experience amongst autistic people.

In school, there is usually at least one teacher we do not like. We do not always understand, while we are young, why this particular teacher makes us extra stubborn or irritable, but they do.

Adults may say: "Maybe it is because of the subject they teach?" and they may very well be right in some cases. But for many of us, looking back, we realize the reason was, actually, that the teacher acted superior.

> "I respond much better when people speak to me as an equal. It is very important that I feel safe and comfortable with the people who give me advice or teach me. If I feel safer and have more respect for the teachers, it is easier for me to focus. I also feel less inclined to be overly sceptical of what they tell me, or to challenge their authority." (Anonymous, personal communication)

Autistic children react very badly to being spoken down to or being patronized. An attitude of "I am an adult, so I know better" or "I am smarter than you" (note, not just saying this, but having the attitude of it!), will be picked up by the child, and met with resistance. Instead, as Scott, an autistic man, wrote to me:

> "Appeal to the child's logic, properly articulate the reasoning behind an argument or the intended purpose behind a task, and respect will be earned in spades." (Scott, personal communication)

Language

There are several parts to the language differences between autistic and non-autistic people. It will be easiest, I think, to describe these separately, although they are not entirely separate issues.

We understand the meaning of a word, not the connotations—which is a learned ability. It can be learned, but it takes time. We use the word with the meaning we understand it to have. This is not necessarily the dictionary definition, though in many cases it will be—even in cases of academic words that a child would usually not know, it is not uncommon for autistic children to have exceptional and advanced vocabularies, especially when it pertains to a special interest.

This then means that we use language in a very literal way and understand it in a literal way. Some do this much more than others, and again, as we get older, this can change. But as children it means that especially metaphors and sarcasm can be difficult, and simple instructions or rules can be misunderstood, often because they are not generalized, as described by Donna Williams:

> The significance of what people said to me, when it sank in as more than just words, was always taken to apply only to that particular moment or situation. Thus, when I once received a serious lecture about writing graffiti on Parliament House during an excursion, I agreed that I'd never do this again and then, ten minutes later, was caught outside writing different graffiti on the school wall. To me, I was not ignoring what they said, nor was I trying to be funny: I had not done exactly the same thing as I had done before. (Williams 1998, p.64)

In some cases, we may view language simply as a tool to communicate messages and ideas, but not so much emotions and social relations. This understanding of language usually comes without the appropriate cultural connotations, and also without understanding the history of certain words or phrases, which means we may sometimes say something very inappropriate, but have absolutely no idea why it is so. It also means we may say something that sounds like a joke to others without realizing why they perceive it as funny.

Many of us do not notice the body language and tone of voice you use to regulate meaning to the same degree or amount of detail (or alternatively, we notice too many details and therefore teach ourselves to ignore them, due to the amount of effort it takes to dissect and translate each detail).

In my opinion, this is the basis of a great deal of the misunderstandings that occur when allistic and autistic people communicate.

As shown in this model, the allistic (NT) person approaches a conversation with not only words, but also their connotations with the (to them) appropriate body language, facial mimicry and vocal intonation, and they expect to see these reflected in the person they speak to.

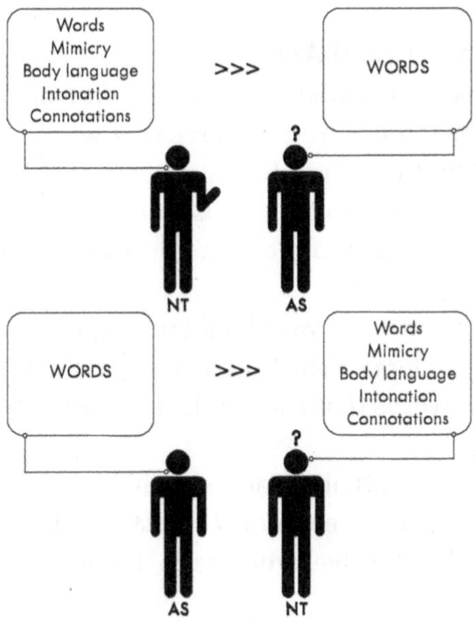

The autistic person (AS) expects all the important information to be in the words themselves and may not even be able to read everything else yet, either due to age and not having learnt yet, or due to not being capable of learning (this part is individual). This means that the autistic person misses a lot of information coming from the neurotypical person, but just as importantly, the neurotypical person expects the autistic person to use body language and so on. in their communication and interprets the communication accordingly—that is, they are interpreting the lack of body language to carry meaning in the same way that the presence of it would have meaning in their own communication. With missing information on one side and assumed information on the other, a great number of misunderstandings can occur in everyday life. Not only between strangers, but also between people who otherwise know each other, because occasionally, each side will forget their respective handicap in communicating with the other party.

A similar concept is the "double empathy problem" as proposed by Damian Milton (2012), and I encourage people to look this up as well.

WHAT DOES THIS MEAN?

First, it means we as autistic people benefit from learning the concept of these things to the degree that we can cope with it. It takes time, but it makes life easier eventually. That is to say, make the information available to us, but do not force us to mask our behaviors or change our communications to that of allistic people.

Second, it means that you should not expect us to know any of this and much less be able to act accordingly. Try as much as possible to use words that convey the full meaning of what you mean to say.

Third, try not to attribute added or hidden meaning to anything we say. We may get emotional and say emotional things that do not convey how we feel when calm, but generally speaking, we do not manipulate and we do not hide behind misleading statements.

This also means that if you ask, "How are you feeling?" you will get the true answer. We will not say "fine" unless we know that this is the culturally expected response. We will tell you how we actually feel—if we know ourselves, of course.

Disclaimer: While comparatively rare, some autistic people can and do learn to lie, especially in cases where it avoids confrontation to do so. Some can also learn methods of manipulation or ways of avoiding certain situations. These are often rudimentary and very obvious, but as with any other population group, some of us are capable of these social skills, even though conventional wisdom says we are not.

Loss of Skills

A frustrating and unfortunately consistent problem for some autistic people is loss of skills. Previously mastered skills may be lost after experiencing severe trauma or long-term stress. I want to reiterate this, as skills do not tend to be lost without causes such as these. I also want to note that this can happen to non-autistic people, although it seems to be rarer.

It is important to remember that the skill is actually lost, and that we are not simply refusing to do these things, though to an outsider it may appear so. In many cases, the skills must be re-learned, just as it had to be learned the first time. In some cases, the skill can be temporarily lost, even over a longer period of time, and the brain will sort of "remember" the skill again, after trauma or long-term stress has been or is being treated.

This can be extraordinarily frustrating and scary to the person who suddenly loses one or several skills, but also to people around them. A part of what makes it frightening is that it is completely unfamiliar: it is not something one usually sees or hears of. But another part is that it can make people nervous as to what other skills might be lost. This is a legitimate concern, but the primary concern should be in preventing future trauma, as that in turn will help to prevent future loss of skills.

Some of the skills we are prone to losing are social, language/speaking and motor skills. If this happens, I recommend focusing first on decreasing any anxiety or depression that may result from the loss of skills and decreasing the stress that caused it, before moving on to re-learning the skill. This is because re-learning a skill is often expressed as being very taxing and at times feeling humiliating as the person recalls having this skill, of course, but simply cannot remember how to do it.

My advice is to avoid re-traumatizing the person through

creating a mood dominated by anxiety about further loss of skills: Do your best not to treat it as a big deal. Rather, this is a fact of life, and one must move on and re-learn the lost skills at whatever pace is reasonable, and, as always, please consult a professional whenever in doubt.

It is also possible to have a temporary loss of skill where, typically in a very stressful situation, we may lose the ability to speak, for example. Once we calm back down the skill returns. This issue seems to have more to do with short-term stress, related to our tendency to react in emotional extremes. Once again, do contact a professional about this as it can become a real issue in life.

The important thing to keep in mind is that losing skills is related to having been faced with serious challenges and traumatic events that one cannot cope with, for one reason or another. It can happen to anyone. It does not mean the person is "weak" in any way.

Furthermore, it is important to remember that the skill can be re-learned, and that the key is to prevent further trauma and severe stress.

Neurodiversity

Due to its classification as a developmental disorder and the difficulties associated with ASD/autism, it has historically been seen as something undesirable. However, in more recent years, autistic people have begun to distance themselves from this way of talking about autism. An example of this is the increasing number of autistic people using that very term—"autistic person"—rather than "person with autism." This carries the message that autism is an intrinsic part of us which we do not feel should be separated from us. It is a part of how we view the world, how we experience it, how we think, and because of that, it is a part of our identity. Not our entire identity, of course, but a part of it.

The idea of neurodiversity, coined by Judy Singer, is that just as there is biodiversity, such that each human is a little different from every other human, there is also neurodiversity. There is no "normal" to aspire to, because every brain is normal and unique at the same time.

For many, neurodiversity signifies the remarkably simple (but also to some people very offensive) notion that the way our minds work should not be stigmatized, should not be seen as dysfunctional or "wrong." Our minds work differently from the "norm," but diversity is good, and this includes diversity of neurologies—ways brains can function.

The neurodiversity movement does not only apply its message to autistic people but also to other forms of differences, such as ADHD. However, since this book is about the topic of *autism,* I will not delve too deeply into that. Suffice to say that neurodiversity is about the world being big enough for all of us, with our differences in thinking, perceiving and acting.

The neurodiversity movement asks that we allow autistic people to be autistic. That means not trying to change our behavior to be less autistic, for example, by teaching (or training) us not to stim. Our autistic behaviors are a part of us, they have purpose for us and they are not "wrong."

It also asks that we make accommodations in society to make it easier for us to exist, in the same way that many places have accommodations for people with different physical disabilities.

As for the other topics in this book, this chapter is not exhaustive in its coverage of neurodiversity, instead providing a short introduction.

Profiles

When talking about autism, we often refer to someone's profile. It really just means "how autism is expressed in this particular person." You will have an idea of it just from knowing them.

The concept of autistic profiles was introduced after professionals discovered how individual autism was, and especially after general gender differences were discovered.

I will give a quick introduction to the general, classic "male" and "female" profiles. I put these in quotation marks, because while they are often spoken about as if there are set gender differences in this way, they are by no means absolute. Girls can have the male or classic profile, so called because those were the traits first discovered and described, and likewise, boys can have the "girl profile." Furthermore, this does not take into account the large number of autistic people who are not cis-gendered. This is to say, we sometimes still use these terms of classic autism and girl profile, but they are wildly misleading and can cause a great number of people to be misdiagnosed or have delayed diagnosis because professionals and carers neglect to see autism when it is expressed in ways that do not conform to the gender stereotypes we are taught to look for.

Note that these introductions will be stereotypical in nature, as this is how they are often taught to professionals, which means some professionals will miss profiles and behaviors that fall outside the expected. However, in the real world, every autistic person is different and so will their profiles and skills be. With this in mind, here is a brief introduction to those stereotypes.

The classic profile describes someone who has little to no interest in social interactions, or seemingly so, or who is socially intrusive and intense to a degree that is uncomfortable for others. Often, it is not mentioned that someone can change back and forth between these two ways of acting, often depending on the company, or shifts in their overall emotional state—for example, someone who has previously been socially motivated can become withdrawn and introverted during stressful periods, after a traumatic experience or due to depression. They are described as having relatively few conventionally expressed emotions, often using either little to no facial expressions, or alternatively extreme ones that are or can seem forced, for example, a smile may look like a grimace rather than a genuine smile. Classic autism/ASD is also often described as having a tendency toward physical, externalized meltdowns, having very few friends at any stage of life, and having a special interest that is unusual both in focus and degree.

Social skills can be learned slowly and consciously, need thorough rehearsal and are non-adaptable, meaning they will only be applied to the particular rehearsed situation and not transferred to similar situations.

The cognitive abilities profile is distinguished by being uneven (meaning someone can score very high in one or several categories, but very low in others, whereas allistic people tend to score relatively even across their profile), which is why some people may be able to study astrophysics at a young age, but never learn to tie their own shoes.

The "girl profile" is very different, though the underlying neurological differences from the norm are the same as in the classic profile. It describes someone who is more interested in socializing, but whose social skills are somewhat superficial when no guide is available. There is a tendency to mimic or copy the behavior of others, even going as far as copying someone else's accent, appearance, mannerisms and interests. There can be different reasons for this, and usually the copying behavior is most apparent in the childhood years, with more adaptable social skills being learned through the teenage and adult years. They will tend to have more friends than those with the classic profile—though still not as many as an allistic peer.

Facial expressions, gestures and vocal intonation will be closer to the social and cultural norm, and the emotional range as well appears more "normal" though it usually is not. Rather, someone with the female profile is more likely to hide extreme emotional reactions if they are in situations where reacting might make them feel very embarrassed. Instead, they "bottle up" the emotions to attempt to avoid the social consequences of expressing them and wait until they are in a safe space to react. Often, this safe space is at home.

Due to the effort they put into socializing and controlling expressions and so on, people with this profile will expend a huge amount of energy analyzing and coping with the social world. All autistic people spend a lot of energy on this, but some individuals with this profile just spend even more. Meltdowns are more likely to be internalized (often called shutdowns), and there can be a higher tendency towards depression, self-harm, anxiety, eating disorders and low confidence, though these are issues for a great number of autistic people.

For those with the female profile, it is likely that a special interest will have a focus that is "normal" or more socially acceptable than what is associated with the classic profile, but that the degree of interest in the topic is unusual. For example, they may like Barbies or boybands like their allistic peers, but their knowledge on the topic is extreme in comparison. They may have the same number of posters of horses as their allistic friend, but instead of merely knowing the breeds, they may also be able to tell you which edition of which magazine each poster came from, and the history of the breed, the physiological facts that differ between them, and so on and so forth.

As with the classic profile, there is often an unbalanced cognitive abilities profile. However, since many people with the female profile are very concerned with appearing normal, they may work extremely hard to cover up the things they are not good at, especially if they are noticeable things like not being able to tie their shoes. They may also only cover them up at school and with other family members, but not care to hide it from you.

An additional profile is the PDA (Pathological Demand Avoidance) profile. It is a very clinical, and perhaps somewhat judgmental, name, and to some extent the name might miss the point entirely. This is a point of contention, but not something to be discussed here as it would distract from the purpose of this book. (I have heard autistic people refer to their PDA profile as 'Persistent Demand for Autonomy' instead, which may help to not pathologize it.) The PDA profile is, in its essence, a profile defined by high levels of anxiety and fear of not living up to the demands made by others or oneself. There is an intense fear of failure which instead causes the child—or adult—to entirely avoid agreeing to meet the demands. To say the least, this profile can be challenging to work with, not only for parents and professionals but also for the person who lives it. The levels of anxiety involved are exhausting and can be related to traumatic stress. Therefore, this is not a profile which is "treated" by treating the anxiety. Rather, managing this profile, for the person with it, is often a lifelong process and requires that the traumatic stress is acknowledged. If your child has this profile, my primary advice is to remember that your child is trying their best to make it through life, even when it seems like they are hiding from it.

This is a quick introduction to profiles and therefore not complete. The point of this section is not to give you a recipe for what to expect, but rather to give you an idea of what professionals expect and can possibly misunderstand—the classic profile is still the most widely known and thus other profiles are often misinterpreted or dismissed—and much more importantly, to make you aware of the wide range of profiles that exist.

Do not expect your child to have one or the other profile. They will not. They will have their own unique profile.

Sensory Sensitivities

Dr. Tony Attwood uses an explanation of the capacity for social interaction that I find extremely useful as the foundation to describe sensory sensitivities. He invites us to imagine the brain as a clearing in a forest. In the center, there will be a plant that represents the social part of the brain. For a person who is not autistic, this plant is a tree. It grows strong and tall, and its branches and leaves take up a lot of space, blocking sunlight from the plants underneath. It uses most of the water and nutrients from the soil. All of this means that the other plants—the parts of the brain that are dedicated to senses—remain small flowers.

The allistic brain sacrifices other aspects to feed the social one.

But for an autistic person, the social plant is a small tree, a bush or even just a flower. It does not keep sunlight, water or nutrients from the other plants, allowing them to grow bigger and stronger. Therefore, autistic people have all kinds of sensory sensitivities. They can be auditory (especially sudden or "sharp" noises and pitch), tactile, visual, aroma, proprioceptive (position and movement of the body), pain (either hyper-sensitivity or hypo-sensitivity, in which pain is not felt as strongly or not at all), temperature sensitivities (again, either hyper- or hypo-sensitivity), and there can also be a mind and body connection issue, which can stem from the same sort of neurological reasons as sensory sensitivities, or it can be a psychological issue, in which case it will usually appear after a traumatic event.

An autistic person can have only one sense that is a lot stronger (or weaker) or they can have several. This means that we experience certain things differently. A taste, smell or texture that is perfectly fine for you may assault our senses. Light changing or vibrating may be a relatively mild annoyance for you, or you may be completely able to disregard it, but it is so overwhelming for us that we are unable to move forward until it has been processed (which, in the case of sensory experiences like vibrating light, we may not be able to do at all).

We all have different sensory sensitivities. The sensory profile is unique to the person and can change over time. Certain things can get better or worse with age or with environmental changes and most often extreme emotional states such as depression, anxiety and stress can mean that we have so little energy left to process the sensory experiences that our whole world seems to collapse.

Coping strategies can be learned, but in times of emotional stress we may not be able to use them. Remember that your child is not making it up or being purposefully difficult. It torments them just as much as it does you, if not more (most often a lot more). Every person experiences sensory sensitivities in their own way, and for that reason it is hard to give one clear description of it. A quote from Carolyn, a woman with Asperger's syndrome, published in *The Complete Guide to Asperger's Syndrome* by Tony Attwood, gives one example:

> "With fluorescent lights it's not only the glare that gets me, it's the flicker as well. It produces 'shadows' in my vision (which were very scary when I was young) and long exposure can lead to confusion and dizziness often resulting in migraine." (email to Tony). (Attwood 2007, p.285)

One aspect that is rarely spoken of when describing sensory sensitivities is that sensitivities can also be positive. For example, there can be certain textures or sounds that we enjoy to such an extent that it can stabilize our moods or even distract us from stressful elements in our surroundings. Most of these are probably unnoticed by those around us, yet not all, as can be seen in this quote by Donna Williams. She describes a positive sensory sensitivity in her book, *Nobody Nowhere*:

> One sound, however, which I loved to hear was the sound of anything metal. Unfortunately for my mother, our doorbell

> fell into this category, and I spent ages obsessively ringing it. (Williams 1998, p.45)

If your child has such a positive reaction to, for example, a food item, the smell of a particular fabric softener or flower, harmonic sound or a certain color or pattern, it can be very useful to encourage using it as a coping mechanism and find ways to use it as positive reinforcement, especially in the early years.

Not everyone has a strongly positive sensory sensitivity, and not everyone has distinct sensory sensitivities. As with everything else, it is unique to the individual. Find out what your child's profile is and keep track of any important changes. You can use this knowledge to avoid the bad sensory experiences and grant extra access to the good ones.

Lastly, autistic people are more prone to a phenomenon called synesthesia. This is when sensory input triggers a perception in a second sense. The most common is when a written word or symbol triggers a color or sound-color, but it may be different things. So, if you discover that your child has this, do not be alarmed. It is harmless (though it can sometimes be annoying for the people who experience it). It is a known phenomenon, and it is, as far as we know, simply the "wiring" in the brain that connects the senses in a way that is relatively uncommon. Allistic people can have this too but are less prone to it.

Social "Languages"

I am often asked why I think autistic people benefit from learning some adaptive skills in terms of communicating with the "allistic" world. There is a short answer and a much longer explanation for that answer.

The short answer is this: It is beneficial to any person to learn to communicate with others to the best of their ability because it helps them get what they need to survive and thrive in the long run.

I will note already at this point that I do not believe that autistic people should be forced to learn these skills, but rather, I believe that the skills are beneficial when learned and used willingly, with intent and reason. This means that it should be the person's individual choice what to learn and when to use the learned skills.

Here is the explanation:

The allistic/non-autistic person uses (seemingly by instinct) all sorts of cues in their communication, such as connotations, vocal intonation, body language and so on. The autistic child (or even adult) uses words primarily, and if we take note of the rest it is secondary to the words. These different ways of engaging socially result in a lot of misunderstandings.

This is where an analogy of languages may be useful. I personally speak only two languages fluently: Danish and English. Danish is a language only spoken by approximately five to six million people in the world, whereas English is spoken by several hundred million people. When I travel the world, the odds of my meeting someone who speaks English are far greater than meeting someone who speaks Danish. Because of this, it is very helpful for me to be able to speak English, and the better I do so, the easier it will be for me to navigate the countries in which

English is the primary spoken language, as well as the countries where it is a second language and where Danish is not spoken at all.

In much the same way that I speak different languages, one could say that I also speak "AU" (autistic) and "AL" (allistic), which makes life a lot easier for me. There are comparatively few autistic people, so being able to speak "AL" makes my life easier. It does not matter if my "AL" skill only goes far enough for me to communicate the concepts of "Hi," "Help" and "Thank you," the skill is still useful. Likewise, it is useful for an allistic person, if they know someone who is autistic, to be able to speak "AU." That way, communication is made easier.

Neither of us have to change who we are in order to communicate better; we only have to learn to translate what we mean. Your child does not have to be someone different in order to learn to speak "AL," but rather, they simply learn some skills to translate who they are, in a manner that more people may understand. This way, they are more likely to get their point across and less likely to be misunderstood in negative ways.

Try thinking of the autistic way of communicating as a separate language or culture and teach us to navigate the "AL" world as you would teach us to navigate any other culture. However, as mentioned, do not force the skills upon your child. Let them know that there is a skill to be learned if they want it.

And to reiterate, when in Denmark, it is also very useful indeed for you to learn to speak Danish—similarly, when you are among autistic people, learning to speak "AU" will benefit you greatly.

Stimming

It is very common to come across this term when navigating the world of information about autism, but for the most part, what you get is a sterile and factual description of what it is: self-stimulatory behavior, such as flapping, rocking, spinning, or repetition of sounds, words or phrases. It is most often a symptom of autism but can also be seen in individuals who are not autistic.

What you are less likely to hear is why we do it, how common it actually is and what it is like.

The sort of stimming associated with autism is usually very obvious to observers. It is either loud or big in some way. But many very common behaviors have the same functions for everyone else that our forms of stimming have for us. It can be a way to try to control emotional response, as a girl with Asperger's describes:

> "I stim when I can feel myself getting sad or angry, to try to stop my emotion from getting too big. I do it to try to control the feeling. It does not always work, especially when someone says something to me that aggravates the emotion." (Anonymous, personal communication)

Another girl expressed that stimming is necessary for her to cope with the world in general:

> "I think I would explode if I weren't allowed to stim. It's like scratching an itch or sneezing. I can't help it and—for me at least—it feels completely natural. I'm a very anxious and sensitive person, and with the world being crazy and overwhelming, stimming helps me cope." (Ellen, personal communication)

It can also be a way to block unwanted sensory input, by substituting our own, more pleasing (to us) and more predictable output. Frequently, this is done by putting our hands over our ears, humming or otherwise making predictable (often constant or rhythmic) noise, or perhaps rocking or hitting/tapping something with our hands. The more physically extreme the stim, the less bearable the unwanted sensory input is likely to be.

With regard to the subject of stimming, what I mean to say is that those who can regulate which stimming method to use will usually, to the best of their ability, use the less obvious, large or loud physical methods when they are sufficient. This means that if it is possible to distract myself from or override the unwanted sensory input by tapping my fingers together or squeezing an object in my hand, then it is not likely I will begin to stim in a way that is painful or harmful. I go through the possibilities starting with the most benign and less painful, and when one "level" of stimming fails to do its job, I move on to the next.

Unfortunately, not everyone has the control or understanding of their own stimming to consciously apply it as a tool, and they may only know a few ways to attempt to override the unwanted input, or it may even sometimes be impossible. As certain stimuli are physically and emotionally unbearable for us, this is when breakdowns often occur.

An autistic man wrote to me this description of being overstimulated; I think he paints such a good picture of the feeling we are often trying to cope with when we begin to stim in more obvious ways:

> "Trying to describe the experience of being overstimulated... It's like any of those old classic cartoon scenes where the character has steam issuing out of their ears and nostrils, their cheeks are red and swelling with the same held breath and their entire body appears clenched, shaking violently in place. But nothing about it is comical." (Scott, personal communication)

An example of sensory stimuli that is hard to bear even for

allistic people could perhaps be having your teeth worked on at the dentist. How do you cope? Do you perhaps try to think of a "happy place" or try to remember a song in your mind to distract yourself? Maybe you grip the arms of the chair really hard with your hands or squeeze your eyes shut? So, what sorts of common behaviors are forms of stimming? Tapping your foot when anxious is an avenue for keeping that emotion in check. Similarly, biting your nails or pacing could also easily be seen as stimming. So really, the big differences lie in whether or not you have sensory sensitivities to deal with and, also, the quantity and form of stimming. Those of us who are autistic do it more often and more obviously.

It can be debated whether there might be a category of stimming which purely concerns creating pleasant sensory input. We can become very addicted to repetitively causing some form of sensory experience, which we find pleasurable, for example touching a certain fabric or hearing specific sounds.

I might be reluctant to call it a stim because the word stimming is often associated with regulating our responses to negative emotions or sensory input, and these would go beyond that definition. However, I am inclined to call these activities "stimming" because they can in many cases be used very efficiently to regulate negative emotions or sensory input, sometimes much more so than other stims. One category these almost always fall into is pleasant sensory "sensitivities," as they are things we react to more extremely than would an allistic person. In this case, however, it's in a positive way.

Terminology and Autism

Over the last decade, the way we refer to and talk about autism has changed a lot and will likely continue to evolve. For this reason, it can feel difficult to keep up. This brief segment will go through a few of the terminologies that are currently, or were recently, in popular use.

Note that in academic or clinical texts you will often find terminology that is outdated when viewed from the perspective of popular language used in the autistic community, particularly online. This is partially because the academic and professional world is slower to update than popular language is, and partially because some academic and professional institutions have guidelines in place for language, and these guidelines are made from a different viewpoint on what terminology is used/needed for, and what connotations are attached to the words.

HIGH-FUNCTIONING VS LOW-FUNCTIONING

Previously, the terms high-functioning and low-functioning autism were quite common. They are still sometimes used in academia.

The general autistic community rejects the terminology, however. The most common reason stated is that high- and low-functioning terms are often applied based on apparent, observed "functioning" judged by professionals or carers around the person. In this sense, the terms really refer to the level of support needs which are perceived by others, rather than the actual internal experience. An autistic person may appear to be coping very well when in fact they are not. This can lead to, for example, a "high-functioning" person not being given the support they truly need because of high intelligence scores or masking behavior.

Another issue is that high- and low-functioning labels are quite static in nature. Once a person is labeled as either it tends to stick, precisely because many people conflate high-functioning autism with things like high intelligence scores, verbal language, masking behavior and less apparent social difficulties. Low-functioning autism is then often conflated with the opposite.

This is a problem because things like verbal language use and masking behavior can be situation-dependent or can fluctuate based on stress levels, but the functioning label will still stick, not changing with the person's current needs.

Autistic people are seeking to introduce the terms high support needs, low support needs or complex support needs, with the acknowledgment that support needs may fluctuate significantly based on situation, current life events, stress and much else. That is to say, support needs are not static, and a support needs label should not be either.

PERSON-FIRST/IDENTITY-FIRST LANGUAGE

Person-first language is recommended—if not required—by most professional institutions around the world at this point in time. Person-first language is when you say "person with x"—it is used with all types of disabilities and diseases. In the case of autism, you would say "person with autism" or "person with ASD."

Identity-first language, on the other hand, would call for you to say "autistic person," putting the identity label first. What this does is to say that autism is a part of the person and cannot be separated from them, as person-first language attempts to do. Autism is not a briefcase that can be put aside or a disease to be cured; it is a part of the person and their experiences growing up. It shapes how they perceive the world around them and how that world meets them. Most autistic people prefer identity-first language these days, and within the autistic community you find identity-first language is used almost exclusively. Others do still prefer person-first language, and this should of course not be ignored.

Professionals and parents largely prefer person-first language, which is the reason it is so much more widespread in academia and clinical work as well as within the media. However, there are examples of identity-first language starting to emerge.

In this book you will find that the language reflects the preferences of the autistic community rather than academia and professional institutions. As an autistic person myself, I do not find either term inherently offensive—rather, the intent or context within which a term is used can be.

In daily life, I recommend asking people which terminology they prefer.

SOME BASIC AND GENERAL TERMS

Back when Asperger's syndrome was still a separate diagnosis in the DSM, it was common for those diagnosed to call themselves aspies. However, the Asperger's syndrome diagnosis being combined with other autism diagnoses, as well as recent information having come out about Hans Asperger who named the syndrome, has meant that the term has lost its appeal for many. Instead, those who used to call themselves aspies will often call themselves autistic, just as anyone else with an autism diagnosis would.

There is also a recent tendency towards neuro-terminology. People with autism and other neurological differences may call themselves neurodivergent or neuro-atypical (the former being more popular in use). The term neurotypical was used for many years to refer to people who are "typically developing." However, in line with neurodiversity, which posits that there is no such thing as normal or typical, many now use the term allistic to refer to non-autistic people.

These terms are meant as neutral and judgment free. It is not bad to be allistic, neurodivergent, neuro-atypical or autistic.

Theory of Mind and Social Reasoning

Theory of Mind (ToM) is a term that is used in describing how good or bad someone is at determining why other people do what they do, how they think, and so on, and using this to predict behavior. In short—how good is my ToM compared to someone whose theory is "average?" The term also includes "theory of one's own mind," meaning: how well do I understand my own mind, the reasons behind my own actions and decisions, and so on.

In autistic people, the ToM skills are said to be decreased and delayed. These skills can be learned, however. For allistics, they develop in early childhood, and they do so intuitively. Generally, people develop these skills at a certain rate, such that you can say that by such-and-such an age, an allistic child should be able to do this or that. There is a test called "The Sally-Anne test" which has been (and is still) used at certain ages to establish the difference between an allistic child's ToM skills and those of an autistic child. The Sally-Anne test uses dolls to act out a story, in which the child watches one doll (Sally) move an item without the other doll's (Anne's) knowledge. The test aims to establish whether the child can distinguish between their own knowledge (that the item has moved) and the knowledge of the Anne doll (who isn't aware of this). What the test will generally show is that an autistic child has more of a tendency to believe that others share their knowledge and understanding of the world, rather than possessing their own, based on separate experiences. This is, in part, what it means to lack ToM skills.

As mentioned, our skills in this area can increase; we can learn a great deal, but the progression and natural learning of these skills will be, to one extent or another, delayed, and without making a continued effort to learn these skills we will not reach a similar understanding of this social skill as an allistic person, even in adulthood.

> "I think I was 12 or 13 before I realized that people's thoughts and reasoning were different from my own. I understood that people were different from me (we did not look the same, we acted differently etc.) but I always assumed that their thinking was the same as mine. That they'd find a joke funny because I did, that they'd like my favorite band (because it was most definitely the best music ever) and that they would come to the same conclusions as me. I had not even considered that others' minds did not work the same way as mine before I got my diagnosis." (Ellen, personal communication)

Especially as young children, we will tend to describe actions much more than thoughts, feelings and intentions, which means that our understanding of situations and people can lack an element, and this is not only very frustrating for everyone close to us, but it is also very frustrating for us. However, our "learned" ToM skills can reach quite advanced levels, especially when we receive help in learning them.

Once we learn the trick to ToM, we can learn on our own as well. Processing time in ToM tasks will generally still be greater than that of an allistic person, even though we can learn to reach the proper conclusions about others' thoughts, feelings and intentions, at least more often than not.

Social reasoning skills and ToM skills are also decreased in stressful situations, so the more people and the more sources of sound, for example, that there are, the worse our skills will be. So, allow us some calm and some time, and make sure that in helping us learn these skills you respect our intelligence. We learn better when we feel smart, just as you do.

It is important to note that some do argue that autistic people do not lack ToM skills, but that autistic and allistic people each have difficulties in using ToM skills to understand one another. I encourage you to look up the "double empathy problem" as proposed by Damian Milton (2012), as this will go into more depth on the arguments which support the notion that autistic people should not be viewed as deficient in these skills.

I will note here that ToM regarding autism has, to some extent, been criticized of late. However, it is important to know and understand what it means and what the general perception of ToM is, as this is something many professionals are taught as fact.

◇ Part II ◇

WHAT WE WANT YOU TO KNOW ABOUT

This book is designed to be read in a "dip-in, dip-out" way, and in Part 2 you can focus on the topics that feel most relevant to you and your family.

◇ Section 1 ◇

Home Life

Food and Dinnertime

See also:
◇ **Sensory Sensitivities** ◇
◇ **Guests** ◇
◇ **School Parties and Birthdays** ◇

Because such a large proportion of autistic people have sensory sensitivities with regard to the taste, smell and texture of food, this is one of the earliest problems many run into. And even if there do not seem to be any significant sensory sensitivities in this area, the social aspects will often show themselves, either at home or at school.

SENSORY SENSITIVITIES

One of the first things that many parents of autistic children will experience is the child's sensory sensitivities. Each child is different and so is their sensory profile. Attempting to explain sensory sensitivity to those who have never dealt with it as a real problem is tricky, but I think perhaps food is a good place to start.

Almost everyone has a type of food they do not like. Some do not like a specific kind of soup or shellfish or vegetable. Others do not like a specific type of meat or perhaps even a specific piece of an animal such as liver and tongue. Whatever it may be, try to picture the type of food you dislike the most. Imagine how it looks, how it tastes, how it smells and how it feels in your mouth. Ask yourself why you dislike it. Is it one element or several? Which ones? The difference between you and your child is that, for them, it is likely not just one or two things they dislike eating; it can be a whole variety of things, all perhaps for different reasons.

For young children, one problem is their inability to explain why they do not want to eat this food, and parents can become frustrated with their child's limited diet and attempt to force them to eat new things. This might work if your child is allistic—I cannot say for sure as I only have a second-hand understand of being allistic. However, I can tell you exactly why it will not be a good idea with an autistic child. These children already feel assaulted by the food they do not want to eat. Whether it is the smell, the color(s), the shape, the taste, the texture...it feels like an assault on their senses. Attempting to force themselves to eat whatever it is can result in becoming physically ill. This can in turn cause psychological trauma. The child may develop general anxiety around food, which can in the worst cases turn into an eating disorder.

If your child does become physically ill, do not interpret this as an attempt to manipulate you. Obviously, I cannot rule it out as a possibility for every single child, but for the most part the child will be so overwhelmed by the attack on their senses that there is simply no room left to consider social consequences—much less actively manipulate others—and this ability in itself is rare in autistic children.

Being unable to explain why you do not want to do something is frustrating. We know that something is uncomfortable, but perhaps do not entirely know why or how, just that it feels wrong. For an autistic child or young person this can be difficult to put into words. The solution we are able to come up with is sometimes just as frustrating to those around us. We may simply say "no" over and over when told to eat or become unresponsive. Those who are capable of crude manipulation may do anything they can to get themselves excused from the table.

If the problem is texture only, the solution is to find the textures that are appealing to the child and do whatever you can to provide healthy options that have this texture. For example, your child may not like the crunchy feeling of chewing vegetables and/or biscuits. Biscuits can be avoided, but vegetables can be manipulated to have many different textures. They can be boiled, shredded, blended, juiced and whatever else you can think of.

Try different things until you find a texture that your child can cope with.

The offending textures may change over time, which also means that previously offending textures may become non-offending at some point, but it may take years and there is no guarantee.

If the problem is smell, color or taste, simply try to avoid the offending item(s) when possible, especially while the child is too young to be taught coping strategies effectively. Consult a professional about when your child is emotionally and cognitively mature enough to do this.

INTEROCEPTION

One thing that may be surprising is that autistic people may not be aware of their need for food. Their body is giving the signals, but those signals are not picked up. This often happens because the person's attention is consumed by an activity and so the signals just do not "get through" to our conscious minds. However, it can also happen due to problems with interoception. Again, the body is sending the signals to tell us that we are hungry, but we do not notice those signals or misinterpret them completely. The interoception issue with hunger also applies to thirst, and so we can become dehydrated because we do not notice or misinterpret those signals.

This is very tricky to deal with because it means we cannot trust our brains to give us the correct information. There are daily consequences, too. The tiredness, headaches and stomach-aches, and so on. you get from being dehydrated and hungry can be experienced as illness, when in fact it can be solved with regular eating and drinking habits. As a parent, it is therefore important that you find ways to make sure your child, even—possibly especially— as a teenager, is getting enough food and fluids.

One way I do this for myself as an adult is to have containers of water that I know are equivalent to what I need to drink in half a day or a day. This way I can track throughout the day if I am drinking enough. With food, a strategy for me is to have set mealtimes, or to use an app (even ones that one would use for calorie tracking) just to note that I have had three meals and some snacks. If it is a calorie tracking app, I tend to have the rule that I ignore the calorie aspect and do not weigh anything, unless there is some specific reason to.

SLOW EATING

One thing that can be frustrating for parents is that an autistic child can very often be a slow eater. This is perhaps slightly less frustrating if you know why, even if you cannot change it. So here are some reasons why autistic people might be eating slowly.

Sensory environment

The issue here is that brain power is used on processing other things than food. Our brains pick up details at odd times, and this is difficult to control. Usually, it gets easier with age, but as a child you have no filter. So, if the light changes—for example, when it is sunny and a cloud blocks the sunlight—the dampening of natural light that occurs is something we notice and focus on. While your brain has learnt to note such details and then ignore them, many of us have to do this "manually," and so it takes longer.

The list of things that can distract us from the act of eating is so long I will not even begin to try to itemize them. Suffice to say, any sensory input that changes will be distracting.

Social environment/manners

Another issue that can cause the process of eating to be slower is if the mind is occupied with doing certain things right, or not doing certain things.

For example, some autistic people love to talk, and once we get started, we cannot stop. If your child is talkative, there can be some difficulty in balancing talking and eating, especially when one considers the rule: "Do not talk with food in your mouth." This is quite a problem if we are really excited about the conversation because then we constantly have to remind ourselves, "No, I am supposed to eat now."

Another issue that arises in this category is eating neatly. If you, as many of us do, have issues with fine motor skills, eating neatly—or just not getting food absolutely everywhere—can be a challenge. Thus, our minds can become so occupied by holding knife and fork right, using them in such a manner that we do not make a mess, that there is not much headspace left for actually eating, or it can simply be that each movement becomes slow and deliberate, thereby slowing the dining process. Eating neatly is quite difficult for any child, but for a child with fine motor skill problems, or general problems with the proprioceptive sense, it is extra difficult.

You may effectively be asking this child to eat in such a way that they are not overly visible, audible, and when they have finished, their plate—and surroundings—should have no traces of eating ever having taken place, as if they were a ninja, completing a task without anyone noticing their presence. That is a tall order for a child with challenges in fine motor skills, social skills, sensory processing differences, and possibly impaired executive functions. There are so many other important things for a child to spend their energy learning, and so, with a crass attempt at humor, I ask you:

Considering your child, their specific profile and their age, think about what the current priority should be—is there something else they should be learning right now, rather than "ninja-eating?"

Analyzing food

A side effect to having sensory sensitivities and the detail focus that we do is analyzing pretty much everything. This includes food. We notice temperature, texture, color, flavor and patterns. If a piece of meat has fat and cartilage, this will be the sort of thing we have to stop and deal with before we can eat the meat, because of the conflicting textures. Fat can taste very different to the meat it is attached to, and cartilage can be almost impossible to chew. Such things, while they may not bother you, are likely items on our list.

Next is planning how to eat the meal. One flavor affects the flavor of the next thing you eat (this may also explain why autistic people, especially in their childhood, will finish eating one type of food before continuing to the next) combined, of course, with the problem that if you mix food items on your fork, then it is not only the flavors that affect each other, but also textures mixing, which then creates a possibly disliked sensory experience.

In short, eating can take a lot of thought.

EATING DISORDERS

Whole books are written about eating disorders and both the reasons they develop and how to treat them. I do not intend to cover this area but merely give a short introduction to it. If your child has or is developing an eating disorder, you must seek specialized help. There are people who work specifically with people who are autistic and have an eating disorder because autistic people may not to respond to traditional treatment methods as expected. Therefore, in treatment of the eating disorder, autism must also be taken into account. Statistically, the autistic individuals most likely to develop eating disorders are girls around the age of 12 to 14. This does not mean they are the only ones who do, however, so please do not disregard any danger signs just because your child is not in this group.

The basis of an eating disorder can come from several sources, and I will quickly outline three root causes that are common in autistic people. And please keep in mind that it might not be one or the other; it can easily be a combination of these. They may seem similar, but just like autism eating disorders are not as simple as once thought, which, again, is why I recommend contacting specialists for help.

As an additional note to the following sections, there are also eating disorders where a symptom is over-eating. Here I am not only referring to bulimia, in which people binge (over-eat massively) and then purge, but also to binge-eating disorder and compulsive over-eating. There tends to be a connection with anxiety and stress. It is important to be aware of these disorders, because there may otherwise be the risk of thinking that as long as a child is eating, there is no eating disorder present. This is not the case.

Inward-reacting

The inward-reacting profile can lead to depression from an early age. It can also lead to eating disorders. The thinking can go: "I am inherently wrong the way I am, but if I change I can be okay." Changing, in this connection, can often be about losing weight, but there is also a variant which focuses on building muscle—looking more masculine or athletic. This is most common in boys. The goal is to look a certain way, and the hoped-for outcome is either feeling better just because you look "better," or feeling better because others will like you more. It is not so much—at first—a need for control, but the idea that looking a certain way will fix things. One aspect of this is also that a lot of autistic people have a really good memory, especially for bad experiences. Louise, a woman with Asperger's who has battled an eating disorder for many years, wrote to me in an email:

> "I wasn't called fat more often than so many others. I just remember it. Every single time.
>
> We are bombarded with images and ideas from the media that speaks a clear language: People with success, people who are capable are slim. How many overweight singers are there? How many actors? In our world skinny equals success and fat equals failure. And for people who perceive things in a literal way and a very black and white way, there is no middle ground." (Louise, personal communication)

There can be a desire to not just be thin, but to disappear. This is not necessarily related to suicidal thoughts but is more about low self-worth. It is about wanting to be invisible to others. If they cannot see you, maybe they will leave you alone. People cannot make demands you feel you cannot live up to if you are invisible.

Control

Experience tells us that the issue of control stems more often from anxiety than from depression. It is still an inward-reacting pattern in a sense, but the thinking is very different. This is less about how you look and more about getting some measure of control of things. Control is the key word.

The thinking can be: "I cannot control anything else in my life, but I can control what I eat." This, then, becomes such a huge focus that controlling, for example, calorie intake and exercise schedules may become a special interest in itself. Having control of something, and keeping this control, can also be addictive if you feel anxious.

The control may also stem from something deeper and concrete, like being afraid of physical changes and trying to control how you look; trying to remain androgynous, keeping a child-like appearance. In this case, the eating disorder will begin at roughly the same time as puberty, and is rooted in the fear of change, which then turns into obsessive control of calories, weight, BMI... numbers. It is about keeping the change under control.

Another aspect of control is using control of food intake as a reward/punishment system for yourself. In these instances, people feel that not being "good enough" can be corrected with eating less.

Copying behavior

This one is a little convoluted. Some autistic children, more often girls, have a tendency to mimic behavior, to copy others. This enables them to "fly under the radar" in terms of diagnosis because their outward behavior can seem "normal" if you do not know what to look for.

However, this tendency to mimic behavior can take over. The popular, skinny girl from school can become a focus to the extent that the autistic girl feels "I want to be like her" or even "I want to be her." Allistic girls can have those same thoughts, of course. This is not purely an autistic thing. Yet for autistic girls (and more rarely, boys), it can become a special interest. It comes from a need to blend in in a positive way. It is not a desire to disappear in the crowd, but to fit into a group. The "skinny-ideal" that society promotes can become a rule for "how to be popular," and so become a part of the recipe or plan for how to become the person they have in their minds to be.

Once an eating disorder goes on for long enough, it can feel like a separate entity with which you have a relationship. You may know it is harming you, but it feels like it is the only thing you have. You can be afraid of letting go of it because you fear you may return to what you were before: weak, alone, fat or whatever else was the triggering factor in your mind. This is one of the things that make eating disorders so difficult to treat.

Louise wrote to me that:

> "The diagnosis [Asperger's syndrome] opened the door to knowledge, a different and healthier knowledge of how I could create order in chaos, structure my life so I could deal with it again."

SOCIAL ASPECT

You can imagine, perhaps, that having to process the colors, textures, tastes and smells of each item, the brain can be quite busy when confronted with food. But there is an added problem in many households at dinnertime, which is the issue of eating together.

Rather than being able to focus solely on the sensory problem the food presents, we are now distracted by people talking, their facial expressions, voice intonations, gestures and emotions. It could be parents correcting siblings or ourselves on how we sit and handle the cutlery or merely having a calm conversation. This means that the amount of information we have to process can exceed our capabilities, depending on the day's events, our age, and so on. The result can be a loss of appetite and if pushed, potentially a meltdown. Of course, no one wants this to happen, so the idea of any coping mechanism is not to have a young child appear normal, but first and foremost to make sure they are receiving nourishment.

Teaching us to sit up straight, eat neatly and socialize during a meal can take place later in childhood or in the teenage years, depending on the individual, but should not be your main priority in the younger years.

There are things that can make the social aspect of eating together less of a strain. Many people—not just autistic—have an easier time conversing about difficult topics while walking or driving. Being beside a person rather than being face to face can lessen the emotional stress. For us, it is this way all the time. If we are not confronted with facial expressions, this means there is less information to process. Even as an adult, I prefer to eat in front of the television. This has nothing to do with the television itself—however entertaining the program might be—but rather that it allows me to keep the social aspect slightly dampened by having people beside me rather than in front of me. I do this especially after a stressful day, in order to not stress myself any further.

Your child might do something similar, even without knowing why they do it, and I would advise that you take their stress levels into account before discouraging this. It can be a good idea to have eating together be an optional thing, possibly in the form of the child opting out when they feel that they will be overwhelmed.

Depending on their age, this can be arranged in different appropriate ways. The key for the child is not to mix the sensory and social difficulties—so if you arrange it in such a way that you can see them, be sure that you are not asking them questions from across the room. "Are you alright?" "How is the food?" and "How was your day at school?" are not appropriate questions to ask during dinnertime. Generally speaking, you want to keep conversation directed at the child to a minimum during this time.

Again, every autistic child is different, and your child may feel happy with conversation while eating, so do take their profile into account.

LUNCH AT SCHOOL

Lunchtime at school can be the most stressful environment the child encounters in day-to-day life. Not only do we have the sensory sensitivities from food and the processing of social cues, but our senses are also challenged from the sound and light in the school environment. Fluorescent lighting is an issue for many autistic people and in the most serious cases it is perceived as an allistic person might perceive strobe lights. I do not think I need to point out that having to concentrate on anything will be difficult under such sensory circumstances. Furthermore, the sound atmosphere in most schools and especially in the school cafeteria can be compared to being in an echo valley or a cathedral with everyone talking at once. Even for many allistic people, this is unpleasant. Many of us have the problem that we pick up the sound from all the conversations, and our brains automatically try to decode all this sound equally. So, keeping up with one conversation over another in such an environment is very difficult, and causes misunderstandings and social and sensory stress. This, again, causes a loss in appetite, general anxiety and meltdowns.

If at all possible, arrange for your child to eat in a smaller social environment, in a smaller room and with non-fluorescent light. This is very important because a child who does not eat during a school day will have to suffer through not only hunger, but also low blood sugar and exhaustion from lack of nourishment. In short, not a good foundation for learning.

A young autistic girl I spoke to about this topic told me:

> "When I don't feel well, I have a lump in my stomach, and then I can't eat anything even though I want to. I try to eat, but after a few mouthfuls it becomes impossible."

It is especially important because if accommodations are not made, we often find ourselves having to make up elaborate ways around our own difficulties, and again this will take away energy from our learning and may increase the risks of getting bullied or even disciplined by the school for breaking rules regarding rooms/spaces we are allowed to eat or be in during breaks and this can end very badly. Scott's story is far from unusual:

> "Still undiagnosed while in school, I took to hiding in a dark, unused classroom, preferably the one I was expected to be in after lunch. Then lunch would be eaten while standing

> over an unzipped backpack; if anyone entered, the food would immediately be dropped inside at which point I would suddenly 'find' the coins needed 'for the vending machine,' displaying them for the startled person to see. This only worked for so long until faculty became suspicious." (Scott, personal communication)

Clothes, Shoes and Shopping

See also:
◇ **Sensory Sensitivities** ◇
◇ **Friends** ◇
◇ **Public Places** ◇
◇ **Self-Identity** ◇

THE SENSORY PART OF CLOTHING

Clothes are tricky because the sensory sensitivities experienced by each autistic individual are unique, at least to some extent. I cannot say therefore that you should avoid certain types of clothes or shoes without knowing your child. Moreover, sensory sensitivities can change throughout a person's life, and so the fabrics or sensations that were unbearable as a child can perhaps become manageable later in life. I will try to give an idea of the general tendencies in sensory sensitivities regarding clothing. Please keep in mind that your child may differ in their profile.

Generally speaking, children with proprioceptive difficulties tend to like tight-fitting clothes with long sleeves and long legs because this helps them know where their legs and arms end and where they are. These same children will be likely to respond well to weighted blankets/duvets (more about these in the last chapter).

Children with no proprioceptive difficulties tend to want less restrictive clothing, and may prefer anything loose fitting, even to the point of looking rather odd. At one point I preferred my boyfriend's hoodie, which was several sizes too big and looked like a very unbecoming dress on me. I did not care, and neither will your child.

In one area, almost every autistic person is similar—comfort comes first. It is okay to look nice, of course, even fashionable. We do not mind looking good, but if it is not comfortable to wear, then, as a rule, we will not wear it.

You will be looking out for hard or scratchy fabrics, pants that are very tight-fitting in the waist (restricting movement and ability to sit comfortably), seams in odd places or that are pressing on the skin. Washing instruction labels can be either cut out or clothing with printed instructions selected instead.

I asked Katinka, a young girl with Asperger's syndrome, what she likes or dislikes about certain types of clothing:

> "Wool is really scratchy, and is very uncomfortable to wear. When it comes to patterns, I really like dots and stripes are okay too, but checkered patterns take a lot of me to look at. It is overwhelming." (Katinka, personal communication)

Many autistic people prefer to wear as few colours and patterns as possible. One adult with autism expressed it as "reducing the sensory noise from my clothing." This means mostly black and white clothing; very dark blue is also often a favorite, no bold or obvious patterns (or even none at all), and no "frilly bits" for the girls.

Again, with age, some things can change, but this is the general rule, so it should give you an idea of what to do. Now, to the actual shopping.

SHOPPING FOR CLOTHES

Stores are confusing places, and there are lots of people. But shopping for clothes and shoes—trying items on, dressing and undressing in a setting where you can hear people around you while in a dressing room—adds an element that just is not much fun at all. So, you are dealing with the stress and noises and your parent waiting to see each item on, to judge if it fits, and so on.

On the topic of dressing rooms and shopping experiences, an autistic woman wrote to me:

> "I, like many autistic people I think, am also a huge perfectionist. I absolutely hate doing things in front of other people if I am not 100 percent certain of them. That includes trying on clothes. I hate having to do it in public, because almost by definition, I am not yet sure of the clothes that I am about to try on. It makes me incredibly uncomfortable to have to do that in a public setting and have to 'admit' when I've been wrong by hanging the non-fitting clothes back on the rack." (Charlotte, personal communication)

On top of that, the tags that are still on the clothing can be very distracting. Even if you might otherwise like wearing the item, the tag can be so uncomfortable that it is almost impossible to tell how you feel about the fabric. As a young child, before you have coping mechanisms to deal with uncomfortable sensory input, it can be very difficult to bear for even a few seconds. Add to this the magnetic alarms attached to clothing in some stores—these can change the entirety of how an item feels to wear, either due to weight (pulling down on one side) or pressure (if it is tight-fitting clothing). This is difficult to deal with as a child but may become easier with age, if and when you get used to it.

Additionally, you may be confronted with staff wanting to help. Of course, they are just doing their job, but the experience can be overwhelming to an autistic person. For some, it is a mild nuisance, while for others it can be a more serious stressor.

Shoes are perhaps even more difficult. Because of the comfort of sameness, we like to wear the same pair of shoes until they are so worn that our toes stick out. But even if you then go and find a pair of shoes that are identical in shape, they will not have been broken in and will therefore feel different. So almost any new pair of shoes is going to feel "wrong" to us, rather than being exciting due to being shiny and new.

My advice is to let go a bit when it comes to insistence on sameness in clothing and shoes. Do not try to pack the wardrobe with colors and accessories. It will only confuse and if the child has any say, might very well never be worn. Go with what they like, and rather than buying the same shirt in five different colors, buy five identical shirts. It could also be nearly identical ones, if they have a motif on them that can be very similar without triggering your child's sensory sensitivities. That way, your child has a clean shirt on, but without the stress of it feeling different and weird compared to yesterday. If this causes trouble at school, teach your child to respond with "No, it is a different shirt than yesterday, but I just like to wear shirts that look the same."

The same goes for all other items of clothing—pants, underwear, socks. Buy identical ones instead of trying to make it fun.

Some autistic girls will refuse to wear dresses, and others will not wear anything else, even if it is far too cold. Again, go with whatever is comfortable for them, and just try to adapt to the weather and climate in some way. Solutions can always be found; sometimes it just takes a lot of trial and error.

However, as Jimmi, a man with Asperger's wrote to me:

> "For many people with ASD, buying clothes and shoes is something we want over with. We generally don't care about fashion, although there are always exceptions to the rule. I do think it can be beneficial for young people with ASD to buy clothes and shoes that are either 'in' right now, or have a more classic style, simply to avoid attention and bullying due to one's clothes. Of course, this does not mean you will not be bullied for other things. It can be good to have help for clothes- and shoe-shopping [from an adult], if you don't have a good friend who wants to go shopping with you." (Jimmi, personal communication)

SUDDENLY WANTING SOMETHING NEW

This happens for us, too. Suddenly, someday, a whim strikes us that we want pink socks instead of black ones. The truth is, very often we did not think it through. Like any other child, we do not know ourselves well enough to realize that even though it is fun today, by lunch tomorrow at school we will want our black socks back on.

Encourage these whims, but make sure there is a back-up plan. That is, put the black socks into the school bag and tell your child, "I am putting your black socks in this pocket of your bag. If you want to switch socks at some point, you can." That way, when the thought hits that "Oh! My socks are pink, I don't want pink socks on anymore!" it does not reach the meltdown stage as easily, because you have already provided the solution.

NON-MAINSTREAM FASHION

Possibly because of living with the feeling that we are always "other," always outside, always strange, many of us are drawn towards fashion choices that are very much outside of the mainstream. We can be drawn towards dressing in a way that resembles characters from a show that is our special interest, or towards a sub-culture that allows us to express the otherness in a way that is attractive for us. This can be, but is in no way limited to, manga - or anime-inspired clothing, goth, punk or metal styles, going to extremes with blending colors— including our hair color—or it can be choosing to dress in historical fashions, such as only wearing 1950s-style clothing or Victorian styles.

For some this is a phase, and for others it is very much something that allows us to express our identity and it may continue throughout our adult lives. It can be a great deal of fun and a source of joy, especially if and when we find others who also love these styles of clothing and with whom we can bond over wearing them.

Lists, Schedules and Reminders

See also:
◇ **Cognitive Abilities** ◇
◇ **Chores** ◇
◇ **Homework** ◇

As a parent, you are going to be doing a lot of listing, scheduling and reminding in an effort to lessen anxiety and satisfy the need for structure and sameness. Having a little control of our world in the form of predictability can go a long way towards our emotional stability and is therefore a big part of preventing unnecessary meltdowns.

> "The world is absolutely draining and overwhelming. Schedules and routines are one of the only ways for me to keep order in a disorderly world. Routines in my daily life give me control in a way I don't get elsewhere and knowing how and when something is happening, in the form of a schedule, minimizes the chance of a meltdown because of an unforeseen event. It takes my brain a long time to adapt. So even if a situation is stressing and uncomfortable, just knowing about it in detail beforehand can make it bearable." (Ellen, personal communication)

SCHEDULES, SCHEDULES FOR EVERYTHING

Your child is given a schedule for school, but it is not complete. You may want to make your own print-out schedule for each day, making sure your child has information on not only which classes and where (which room), but which teacher. You want to fill in whether they take a bus or train to and from school or if they are being brought and picked up. What is for lunch? The more information your child has ahead of the day, the easier it is to get through.

For evenings and weekends, it is more of a judgment call. Does your child feel comfortable not having a schedule at home? Do they maybe need unscheduled time? If you do have a schedule at home, and it says dinner at 6pm, then dinner may have to be at 6pm exactly, depending on your child's profile. But really, when it comes to being in a safe place, which home is, some autistic children function very well without schedules, so try it out and find what suits your child best.

For extracurricular activities, playdates and family get-togethers, there should be some amount of schedule as well, especially if your child is feeling anxious or stressed. It should specify when you are leaving home, when you are supposed to arrive, estimates for what times meals will take place, estimates for what time you are going home, and so on. Again, this all depends on how detailed your child needs it to be—some children need very little detail, others need everything specified.

It is important to observe your child and adjust your use of schedules to fit their needs—for some children, lots of advance warning may be helpful; for others this could be a source of anxiety. Test different approaches and see what works for your family, and don't forget that your child's need for schedules may also very well change as they grow older. There can also be sudden changes in times of anxiety, depression and stress.

RITUALS, ROUTINE AND HYGIENE

The child often develops many rituals of their own. These rituals can become a bit of an obsession, but do not worry unless the rituals start to control their lives. You probably have a certain order in your morning routine too, and you probably do not even think about it.

They may want the cereal box in a specific place on the table or want to wear or not to wear certain colors together, even without this having a basis in sensory sensitivities. It is just a little thing that makes them feel good to do a certain way.

However, other routines and rituals may have to be established by you: for example, providing the order and checklist for them to dress themselves. Remembering to check which way the shirt goes, and how to identify this, and so on.

They may also need a routine/checklist in the shower. They may forget the body wash or shampoo, so this needs to be established early on, perhaps as some sort of ritual which can become so well practiced that hopefully they will eventually no longer need to think about every little thing.

One very important point has to do with dental hygiene. It is very common to have sensory sensitivities about our teeth and gums. Many of us have a rather extreme dislike of cleaning our teeth either because we find the brushing sensation or the taste of toothpaste highly uncomfortable.

Dentists advise that parents check their children's tooth brushing, or even redo it after every time, up to around age 12. But your child has autism. You do not stop at age 12. Until your child has caught up in terms of executive functions to the extent that they can remember and do this correctly every time, you do not stop.

I stress this point because some children have been known to simply stop brushing their teeth once their parents stop checking, and once the routine drops they do not pick it up again. This means your child could suddenly decide at age 15 or 16—when you think that now, surely, they can manage themselves—to stop brushing their teeth because they do not like it, and a few years later, you start seeing the evidence.

So, any ritual or routine that has to do with something your child does not like doing should be checked, especially when it has to do with their long-term health and well-being.

For as long as it is possible, try to make it a calm social activity: for example, brush your teeth together in the mornings and evenings. Once the child becomes older and perhaps does not find it fun to do together anymore, find some way of checking it without intruding too much on their sense of self. Perhaps there are apps or electric toothbrushes that record how long someone spends brushing their teeth. Do some research and see what is available in your country.

LISTS

Lists are especially useful to combat our problems with planning and prioritizing. As a young child, I used to have meltdowns at the mere request that I tidy my room. It was not that I did not want to tidy my room, it was that I had no idea where to start, where to end, or to what standards it should be tidied. Lists help incredibly. Even now, as an adult, I make a list of what needs doing when I can no longer distinguish beginning from end. Then, when I am done with everything on the list, I can see if anything else needs doing.

While your child is young, they will need you to compile the lists, but as they grow older you can include them in the process, thereby teaching them a skill they will need throughout their whole lives.

REMINDERS

Even with all these lists and schedules, we still need reminders sometimes. And it is hard to find a balance between reminding your child too many times and too few. You know your child best but try to remember that their needs and abilities change (and hopefully improve) as they get older, so when at age seven, they might need ten reminders leading up to an event, they might need four by the time they are twelve. Or they might need one.

Due to the individual nature of autism and its expression, it is very hard to predict correctly what sort of maturing and learning curve you will see. But to the extent that it is possible, you should try to adapt to it. A good place to begin implementing reminders is if there is a major event coming up. Give the first reminder a week ahead, then five days before, three days, two days and finally one day before. The reminders should not be big or dramatic in any way; they should be calm reminders. It's also preferabe that they're visual, so if possible, have a calendar hanging somewhere within easy reach of your child, and with them, cross out each day leading up to a major event. They may also enjoy crossing the days out every day, in which case you can do this with them and then calmly remind them when there is a certain number of days to an event. Such a calendar can also be color-coded. I find that color-coding works very well because of our visual way of thinking. Let your child choose which color school should be, which color for an activity, playdates, family events and so on. Have pens in each of those colors close by so that they are ready for adding things to the calendar.

Chores

See also:
◇ Cognitive Abilities ◇
◇ Sensory Sensitivities ◇
◇ Pocket Money ◇

It is good for children to participate in the home. It makes them feel accomplished (especially if complimented and rewarded), included and "grown up." But there is a big difference in which instructions to give to an autistic child compared to an allistic one.

Most of the problems that will be encountered here are problems that arise due to delayed or impaired (different) executive functions. I mention these in the Cognitive Abilities chapter.

It is important that you understand that your child is not stupid or rebellious; it is simply that their brain processes information differently, and that their ability to govern prioritizing, planning, time management and impulse control is different, and that they need tools and good instructions from you to learn strategies.

One overall piece of advice is that you must make your expectations clear. We cannot meet them if we do not know them. This means that communication is key.

THE LANGUAGE BARRIER

"Would you take out the trash?" is a phrase you would expect most children to understand. But if you live with someone who is autistic, especially someone who is not aware and has not been taught to understand this phrase in the way it is meant, you are most likely to hear a "yes" or "no" answer, and then the trash will stay exactly where it was. Why? Because we understand what is said, not what is meant. We might be confused by the question because it lacks a description of the specific circumstances under which we would or would not take out the trash, and therefore we cannot answer. Alternatively, we will make up the rest of the question ourselves, the most likely version of which will be "Would you take out the trash, if I asked you to?" to which we then either answer "yes" or "no," but you still have not actually asked directly so no action takes place.

This problem of understanding will continue until the person has learned to understand such phrases—yet do not expect that once we have learned one we have learned them all. It does not work that way, unfortunately. Additionally, even if the question is understood, an autistic teenager may still rebel, in which case you are most likely to get the "no" answer. We have these phases, just as allistic people do.

The way around this is to learn how "autistic logic" and the "autistic language" work, and to work with them rather than against them. Instead of asking "Would you...?," you can say "I need you to... before..." or "...because..."

Fill in the blanks, it can be anything. What is important is that you have stated what you would like them to do and before what time. Optimally, there should be several reminders if it is not a standing agreement, and the child has the executive function ability to remember and initiate the task themselves. Also, consider that your child may need to be told a very specific time for when to do things, otherwise they may get confused or have a very hard time making the choice for when to do it—even within a relatively short timeframe. It depends on how autism affects your child. Doing chores is a routine that needs to be built and maintained like any other. There should be clear instructions on what to do and preferably you should show the child how to do it the first few times and then watch them do it, so there is no doubt as to the chore's scope.

Include details in the description and if your child is good at listening to explanations, then do so as you are showing it. Otherwise, write it down in detail. If there are many steps then make a list of the order in which things should be done to eliminate any possible confusion, which may otherwise lead to feelings of inferiority and subsequent meltdowns. Many autistic people do not learn through imitation in the same way that allistic people do, which is why explaining while actively showing them, being there to teach, is so important.

Usually it is also good for the child to have a chart to check off once the chore is completed. Such a chart could be a physical one somewhere in the house, or it could be an app, depending on what your child works best with. This will give a sense of achievement. When they check the box they are done, and they can feel good about having helped out.

VISUAL AND WRITTEN INSTRUCTIONS

If we have never done something before, we can have a hard time following verbal instructions, especially if these are given before the task is performed rather than during. There are things you can do to teach your child autonomy in performing a task at home . Be aware that the way they are taught to perform the task is likely to be the exact way they will perform it every time, so if you want your child to have different options for how to do it that flexibility should be worked into the instructions. For example, write it down for us, step by step. This should be done in a point or list form, in the correct order. Do not leave anything out. Include every detail that matters to the task being completed correctly. If your child has a hard time following the instructions, it usually means they are not detailed or concrete enough. Another good way to teach your child a task is to show them. This does not necessarily mean that you should leave out the written instructions; it is good to combine the two.

Do the task you want your child to do while they watch and tell them what you are doing—with as few extra words as possible. If you are showing them how to wring out a cloth, for example, do it first, and let them feel how wet it should be for doing this particular task. If you have taught them to wipe off dust, and you now want to teach them to wash a floor, the cloth is different, and how wet it should be is also different. Show them the difference; do not expect them to know.

After you have shown them, watch them do it. Make it a moment of teaching, not a "I'm-watching-to-make-sure-you-can-do-it-right" thing. They should not be afraid of making a mistake when you are watching. Once they have the routine down, let them do it on their own.

RIGID THINKING

An element of the autistic mind is rigid thinking, the "one track mind." This means that once we are doing something, it can be very easy to keep going, forgetting everything else. It also means that if there is a set of instructions to follow to do a task, and something makes it impossible to follow said instructions, we get stuck. We simply do not know what to do. For example, if you keep a certain brand of a cleaning product for cleaning the sink and you have shown your child how to clean the sink with it, but if the brand changes the look of the product or you switch to a different product, you may have to let your child know again which product to use. If the tools for a task are relocated, or you get new ones, your child may have to learn again which tools to use and how. It will take time for them to adjust to the new tool because it might be longer or shorter or feel different to the touch. If it is a vacuum cleaner, it might sound different.

The order and the way in which things are done cannot be expected to have any degree of flexibility. Your child has learnt to do this chore in this way using these products and tools in that order, and they may not be able to deviate from this routine.

This also means there is no quick way to fold laundry or wash the dishes. It will be done right, or it will not be done at all.

Likewise, if you send them shopping, the shopping list might say "butter" but not which kind. If the store is out of the usual brand of butter, the particular size of package or perhaps the packaging has changed, your child may get stuck and not know what to do. They will not think to just get a different size or brand. If you send them for fresh potatoes and there are none, your child may very well get stuck as well. They will not be likely to consider frozen goods as an alternative, so it will be good to specify alternatives that are acceptable or instruct them to call home if there is a problem. These types of conversations with your child will help teach them to think about alternatives and to problem-solve.

SENSORY SENSITIVITIES

With regard to the type of chores your child does around the home, please remember that they may have sensory sensitivities with, for example, vacuum cleaners, as it is not uncommon for the sound to hurt our ears. Likewise, the sound of other household machines may be an issue, or the smell of particular cleaning products. The tactile feeling of certain types of cloths or wearing rubber gloves may be disturbing to a point that you either need to find a different solution, or not assign this particular chore to your child. Please take this into account when choosing which chores for them to take on. They should feel included and valued, not punished. They may become less sensitive to something as they age, but it may also continue to be a problem through adulthood. If you do not see it changing in their teens, you may want to search for other ways for them to do a particular chore, to help prepare them for living on their own.

With some things, there will be strategies or alternatives available. For example, cleaning products which are perfume free can remove the distress from certain smells or wearing noise-cancelling headphones—and possibly listening to music—while vacuuming can make the noise bearable for some. This is to say, do look for ways that sensory sensitivities can be worked around. Sensory sensitivities do not get better with exposure, so trying to "get over it" will not work, regardless of how important it is. However, there are sometimes ways that we can avoid triggering the sensitivities entirely, and this will be a very useful thing to learn how to do.

Discipline

See also:
◇ Amygdala and Emotions ◇
◇ Social "Languages" ◇
◇ Meltdowns and Shutdowns ◇

When it comes to discipline and child rearing, there are some pitfalls you may not expect. Because we process things differently, otherwise mild punishment may become difficult for us to cope with, or it may take a lot more for us to understand what exactly angered you.

Naturally, you want to do what is best for your child and I wish I could present a list of pure facts for you to apply easily. However, as with everything else, we are so very different from one another, and you are often the person who knows your child best. I hope this chapter helps inspire you to consider different ways of approaching discipline and rules in the home.

NOT UNDERSTANDING WHAT I DID WRONG

One of the issues with any type of discipline is that it cannot work if the child does not understand what they have done wrong. Due to our difficulties with generalizing, we may misinterpret rules in ways that seem strange to the outside world. For example, a rule which says "Do not throw your jacket on the floor" may result in the jacket ending up on a chair instead, or on top of our school bag. Indeed, it may even result in the jacket being gently laid on the floor, rather than being thrown, which may be very frustrating to you as a parent. Likewise, it may be difficult to understand, if not specified, that a rule which applies in one place may not apply somewhere else. An example here may be that the dog is allowed on the couch at home, but at a friend's place they do not allow dogs on the furniture. When the friend's parents get upset about me inviting the dog onto the couch, I may not catch the hint.

It can get even more confusing if different rules apply in the same place but not on all days. At the dining table, I am allowed to use my tablet to de-stress, or perhaps leave the table when I feel the need, but when a family member is angry with me at Christmas for doing the same thing, it will be a complete surprise to me.

On the other hand, we may also not understand that a rule should be generalized to all situations. If we are told not to pick our noses, we may only apply that rule to that specific situation and proceed to do it on a different outing, in different company, or even in a remarkably similar situation because we simply have not understood that the rule should be applied more broadly.

Lastly, it is important to remember that children, especially when young, have not developed the ability to connect cause and effect over long periods of time. This ability is something that develops as we age, and at different rates for each person, so I cannot tell you specifics about your child. However, it means that any discipline, whether this be a time-out or a stern talking-to, may not be related in our minds to the actual thing we did wrong. It is too long gone in our memories and no longer really applies. Even if we are told immediately, there is also the possibility that we may forget what we were told. This happens to everyone sometimes, some more than others.

...BUT THE RULE IS STUPID!

There are also rules that are quite simply stupid, in our estimation. These will differ from person to person, but generally autistic children may be unhappy with rules which seem unfair in some way, or which defy our logic.

You may consider a rule in which a child two years older is allowed to go to bed later. The autistic child may not consider this age gap a factor which should cause the rules to differ between them and the older child. It can be very difficult indeed to explain to them why this rule actually makes sense or is fair. Be prepared to try, however, because such rules may be questioned with fervor.

There may be a desire to prove to you that a rule is stupid or unfair, in which case you may have a child who actively disobeys, but it will likely be aimed at a specific rule and with a specific purpose. Rather than using discipline, consider speaking to the child to understand their point of view, and either compromising or finding a (to the child) better way of explaining why this rule is in place. Remember autistic logic plays a key role in this sort of communication.

> "Whenever I was asked to do something as a child, I used to ask 'Why?'. I wasn't trying to be defiant, provocative or misbehave. I just didn't understand why it had to be done right now, why I should do it instead of my sister, why it should be done in this specific way—never mind all the 'How?' questions! There was so much I didn't understand and my questions were endless! But when I asked 'Why?' it usually resulted in an immediate scolding. And when the adults yelled at me, I defended myself by yelling at them. And yelling absolutely didn't help to get my questions answered..." (Katrine, personal communication)

WE TEND TO WANT TO DO WHAT IS RIGHT

Importantly, please remember that autistic people tend to be highly concerned with justice and doing what is right. This can be true even when we are feeling ill, anxious, mentally exhausted or otherwise unwell.

> "I used to suffer from terrible nightmares which would leave me highly anxious and stressed the following day. I would be on the verge of a panic attack. Despite this, I remember only one occasion where I stayed home from school. The thought of missing class or being noted for my absence made me feel

> like a bad person. It was inconceivable. Duty was, and still is, very important to me." (Andie, personal communication)

The rule that you are supposed to go to school can convince us to go, and to stay, at school even to the point where we are incapable of functioning afterwards. Likewise, we may follow rules that are uncomfortable for us to follow, merely because we have been convinced that the rule is ethical or correct.

We may—or may not—be convinced that looking people in the eye, shaking someone's hand, is good because the other person perceives it as respectful. When we have learned that shaking hands is correct, and the other person instead expects a hug, this can make us uncomfortable, not only because of the added intimacy, but also because it breaks with the rule we are comfortable with.

Children, especially young children, may attempt to conceal from or not inform adults if they have been unable to follow a rule. This will be emotionally uncomfortable for the child. If they have been told not to get their clothes dirty because they are going to an event later, and they have accidentally sat on something that stained their clothes, or maybe they have gotten a stain from a marker on it while drawing, they may seek to hide it rather than inform you. This can be out of embarrassment, or simply not knowing how to handle the situation.

Additionally, if what they have sat in was wet, such as remnants of a puddle from rain on a bench, or say, a bird dropping that they did not notice, they may also be physically uncomfortable due to the sensory aspect.

So, the child may not know what to do, as there are no rules/information about what to do in such a situation; they may be embarrassed or afraid of making adults upset/angry, and simultaneously be coping with sensory discomfort.

This is all to say that even if we have broken a rule, we have often tried our best not to, or breaking it may have been accidental, and we may not know how to handle the situation afterwards, once we realize we have broken a rule. And sometimes, this is really punishment enough.

DISCIPLINE CAN HAVE A DIFFERENT EFFECT THAN YOU ARE HOPING FOR

Discipline may affect us in ways that are unexpected and even adverse, even when it would be appropriate for other children.

First, as with so many other topics, be mindful of sensory sensitivities. Any discipline which includes us being exposed to an uncomfortable sensory environment may cause us to be entirely focused on the sensory input rather than the lesson we are supposed to take home. We may be so overloaded by the sound of an angry voice that we cannot hear the words, for example.

Likewise, emotional contagion can become an issue. If you as a parent are angry in the situation, we may unintentionally mirror the emotion, or we may feel that you are angry and become overwhelmed and again, not be able to focus.

Forced eye contact, even if you feel you need to see that your child has listened and understood what they have done wrong, can cause anxiety to the level of causing overload. This can lead to meltdowns or shutdowns, and will not contribute in a positive way to your child's understanding of their actions.

If we do not understand the rule we have broken, we will only learn that adults become upset at random and that they cannot be trusted, or that they expect us to know things we do not. If the rule is stupid, then the discipline makes as little sense as the rule, and we may become even more focused on finding a way to change it.

For any discipline to teach us what we need to learn, the situation must be calm, the rules must make sense and so must the discipline—if it is out of proportion, it may again teach us the wrong lesson or only serve to make us afraid.

It is important to discuss corporal punishment. By now, it is generally acknowledged in psychology and pedagogy that this form of discipline has many negative consequences. Many who have grown up with this form of discipline will say that it did them no harm, and I do not wish to negate any single person's experience. However, studies do show that corporal punishment can put children at a higher risk for developing emotional and behavioral problems. Children with ASD are already at an increased risk for developing anxiety and depression, and adding further risk factors will only put your child in a worse position when it comes to their mental health.

Disciplining when a child is aggressive, when they are upset, is not recommended. Not only is this likely to be the time when you are also upset—in which case the emotions may amplify each other—it is also a time when the child's ability to think and learn is compromised. In the situation, the most effective strategy may be space or reassurance. The child may not be aware of what they have done wrong if it has been done in a state of high emotion, and will be better able to reflect and learn from it once calm.

Pocket Money

See also:
◇ Chores ◇
◇ Friends ◇
◇ Special Interests ◇

When it comes to money, several difficulties can arise. They are often of varying gravity , and some can overlap.

CONCEPTUALIZING THE VALUE OF MONEY

This is difficult for many, if not most, children. For autistic people, money can be such a vague idea that we have no clue what to do with it. The main problem is usually if we cannot properly visualize money or grasp the concept of how much something is worth and why.

This is especially true in this age of credit cards and internet/phone transfers. As an adult this may result in a lack of control over money, massive debt and overspending combined with no clear idea of the consequences, which means that the consequences sometimes are very dire indeed before we realize there even is a problem. And then we have to learn very quickly to control money, and to do so under problematic circumstances.

Naturally, I recommend teaching your child about money, value and budgeting. Use cash if you can, or faux cash such as Monopoly money, not just numbers written down; we might be able to understand such numbers, but for many they do not truly hit home. Introduce your child to concepts of budgeting. It does not have to be a full budget, of course, but when they have a small amount of pocket money, talk to them about how much it is and what can be bought with it. Talk to them about what could be bought with twice as much or ten times as much, thereby introducing the concept and idea of saving for something, and then discuss the concept of saving money for next week or even just tomorrow, and the benefits of that. This could be done by playing a pretend game in which they use their money to buy a number of edible items that they really enjoy, for example, candy or fruit. Have the physical money present for the game, and make drawings representing purchases and items, or if you have the items they want to buy with their money, use those. Have them pretend to spend all their money buying candy or fruit, and then discuss what will happen if they eat it all now, or if they save some food or luxury (candy) for later. Then play the game where they only spend, for example, half of their money or a quarter of it. Talk about how much money they have left and what they could do with it.

When they are older, introduce concepts of rent and paying for electricity, water, phones and internet to prepare them for the expenses which are part of adult life. Also introduce the concepts of insurance and taxes. Make sure you take your child's level of maturity into account more than their age. If possible, either give your child access to the family budget so they can see much is needed to run a household, or have them create their own budget with your help. Having a budget for their pocket money, where they have to save up money for an item they want to buy, put aside money for Christmas gifts and (symbolically) pay for food, can be very helpful in teaching them to account for expenses throughout the month and year later in life. Once again, cash is a very valuable tool for teaching, as it is a visual and physical form of currency, rather than digital, which can be very vague and difficult for us to visualize as something concrete.

Even as an adult, I still prefer cash as a method of controlling my day-to-day spending, both when it comes to groceries and my "allowance." Having control of my spending when it is solely digital is very difficult, and it is simplified greatly with cash. When I can physically see and feel how much is left, it is no longer vague, and I am able to pace the spending on daily living expenses much better.

One way to make it easier digitally could be creating spreadsheets, however this will only work for those who find it interesting or fun, as it does involve a bit of "work."

EXTREME GENEROSITY

While autistic people have a very firm grasp of the concept of personal property, they are also likely to be very generous. As children and adolescents, they can be prone to inviting friends to the movies and to cafés to please friends and maintain friendships, without realizing how much they are spending, and without considering whether these friends ever do these things in return. The absence of reciprocity can often be excused or "waved off" by the autistic person due to low self-worth and the desire to be liked, not recognizing it as being perhaps exploitative or realizing how imbalanced the friendship is in this regard. (An important note here is that friends can come from very different financial situations and as a result, what might normally be considered over-generosity on one child's part is more reflective of them having more resources available. The friendship can still be a close and reciprocal one regardless.)

If someone asks for a loan for food or a bus ticket, your child is more likely than the allistic child to simply grant the loan without considering whether this person is ever going to pay them back, or if this person is even a friend of theirs.

Your child is also likely, due to this naivety, to fall for scams. These include anything that promises a payback—like the scam emails that say you have inherited and you will be paid after you give a certain amount of money, or anything that threatens bad consequences, like the ones that say you have committed a crime and have to pay a fine. They are also likely to play the lottery or to gamble, honestly believing that at some point it will be their turn to win, because the concept of odds is something we either understand very well or not at all.

As your child grows older, talk about each of these things and what to do and why. It is important to teach them to protect themselves, but to avoid encouraging them to be overly sceptical of people's intentions. You do not want to teach them to have negative expectations of everyone, just to keep their guard up against predators and scams. You also want them to know that it is perfectly okay to want to do something nice for your friends, but to know the difference between when it is your own idea to do something and when friends might be trying to coerce you into doing something.

SPENDING ON SPECIAL INTERESTS

This is something that can truly get out of hand. Even the financially aware individual can get caught up in their interest and want something for it so much that they cannot stop themselves. Some autistic adults have wound up in immense debt because their spending on special interests was so out of proportion to their actual financial situation.

When it comes to the special interest, there can also be a strong lack of priorities. The autistic adult may stay within budget, but not prioritize in healthy ways, sometimes opting for only one meal a day, or consciously spending less money on water, electricity, insurance or health care in favor of having more money for their interest. This is one of the reasons why it is so important to teach the concept of money and its value early on, and to train awareness of it as a skill. The point is not to discourage the individual from ever spending, but to find the balance between wishes and a healthy, sustainable reality. Unfortunately, while rare, there are cases where autistic people will actually begin stealing from others in order to finance their interest. This may happen when they feel they have no other options left within their own economy and because the special interest can become such an obsession that nothing else matters. If you see signs of this, I would advise you to contact a specialist about this problem. Even if you think it is expensive or it is money you do not have, I would argue that once this spiral begins, the cost of almost any amount of therapy will pale in comparison to the fortune that can be spent and the troubles that can result from this sort of behavior. Get help sooner rather than later, and again, educate your child or adolescent as much as possible about money as early as possible, and encourage rational thinking when it comes to this aspect of life.

There is also the flipside, where lack of control over everyday spending means that you cannot afford the things you want the most. Signe, a woman with Asperger's, wrote to me:

> "I've probably always been good at spending money. On the other hand, I've also always tried to avoid it. It just never worked. Oddly, it's made my way of spending money very backwards. I have a hard time spending on things I really want, that have to do with my interests, probably because it is usually more expensive things, but small things I can spend lots of money on, as long as they are small amounts." (Signe, personal communication)

This is something that can make us profoundly miserable if we do not have humor about it. Once again, I suggest cash as a possible way of controlling spending. Self-irony can also alleviate the situation, if not financially, then emotionally.

MONEY AS A SPECIAL INTEREST

This can be (almost) as harmful as overspending. Once again, food, electricity and heat will be ignored in favor of the interest, but in this case, the interest is saving and keeping money. Think of it as collecting money rather than stamps.

The behavior will be scrooge-like. The person will always go for the cheapest option and never buy anything they do not need. And when I say need, I mean need as in "for survival" need. This may come in varying degrees of severity, but at the most extreme end, we are talking about a behavior where they will be wearing six shirts and cover themselves with blankets rather than turn on the heat. Of course, their bank statement will look absolutely beautiful, but their life will not be. Again, seek out a specialist and encourage rational thinking and balance. You may want to settle for being happy with slightly less rational behavior than you would otherwise be. Focus on getting them to a point where their lives are reasonably comfortable and they are living in a healthy way; that is, convince them to at least turn on the heat and eat enough to sustain them. Try to teach them early on about the social consequences they are likely to face from not sharing with others. This can be done through roleplaying and Social Stories. They may not agree with what they learn, or care, but at least they will be aware.

Some autistic people have a naturally healthy understanding of and attitude towards money which enables them to have great control of their finances and build their own fortune from a young age. They can be good at investing (and they are likely to put great effort into educating themselves and researching each investment), and they can turn it into a career.

ENTITLEMENT

This problem is related to black and white thinking and language. If your child is used to getting x pocket money every week or month, and your situation changes so that the amount has to decrease, your child could well react with a sense of entitlement—basically, an "I have always gotten x amount of pocket money, so I am supposed to get x amount of pocket money" type of mindset. Here it is not so much rational thinking that causes the problem, rather it is lack of nuanced thinking. It is best to prepare the child for the change a good while in advance, if possible, and talk to them in an age-appropriate way about why there will be a change.

Homework

See also:
◇ Cognitive Abilities ◇
◇ Lists, Schedules and Reminders ◇
◇ School and Class ◇

There are so many aspects that make homework a challenge for autistic people. We learn differently, perceive differently and think differently, so we do not always understand the problems we are supposed to solve, or we may not interpret them in the way they are intended.

HANDWRITING

Some autistic children will find handwriting quite easy. These are often the ones who also have skills in drawing and painting. However, due to the general tendency toward fine motor skill problems, handwriting can be a serious issue. Holding a pencil and making our hands create letters and numbers can be incredibly frustrating, and much more so because it is often combined with a need for perfection. I remember how I would erase and rewrite single letters and numbers, or even entire words, because they did not look perfect. It felt like a failure every time I did not make it look pretty enough, and obviously this also meant that it took much longer for me to complete my homework than it should have. So, having to learn to write at a young age is likely to be a grueling task, filled with tears and meltdowns.

The solution to this is rather simple, if the school is willing to cooperate. Allow your child to type instead. Let them focus on solving the written assignment rather than being endlessly frustrated by their own handwriting. It is not a productive use of energy or time if your child becomes so sad about their handwriting that they cannot complete their assignments, and hopefully the teachers and school can see this.

DISTRACTIONS

The environment needed to get through homework is usually rather spartan. You will want to eliminate as many sensory distractions as possible: consider both desk and chair, light, sound, temperature and smells. Make this an environment that is focused only on the task ahead.

If you have the room for it, try having a specific desk only for homework, so that in your child's mind there is no other activity that can be indulged in at this desk. They should not be distracted by thoughts of drawings, or their colored pencils being right next to them.

ASKING FOR HELP

We sometimes find it difficult to remember we can ask for help.

When we are trying to solve a problem, we are so focused on that task and on trying to shove away the feeling of frustration that comes from not succeeding, that we forget to even consider that someone else may have the answer. It is simply not a natural course of action for us.

Another problem is that we may not even realize when help is needed. For example, many written assignments are phrased by the teacher to mean one thing, but we, being literal thinkers, understand it quite differently. So, we end up solving a different task from the one that was set. And we have no clue that we are actually in need of assistance, because we do not know to check for such misunderstandings.

So, your job, and the teachers' job, is to introduce the concepts of asking for and receiving help, and to make doing so a positive experience. You can do this through setting up short and simple roleplaying games or writing Social Stories about asking for help, receiving it and the problem being solved. These should also include how to ask for help politely and thanking the person who provided help.

Social Stories are a social learning tool created by Carol Gray. You can find more information about Social Stories and how to make them on carolgraysocialstories.com.

After this, you must make sure there is access to help, and talk to your child's teachers about how you have instructed them to ask for help; you also need to stress how important it is that your child has good experiences of asking for and receiving help at school.

LEARNING STYLES

There is a lot of debate about learning styles and how to apply them, and some even question if there is such a thing as a learning style. The fact is that autistic people tend to be very visual thinkers, and generally, the track record for learning and retaining information provided visually to us—in the form of images, not text—far surpasses that of being taught through audio or text only.

However, we are all different, so do not take this as the last word. This is merely a suggestion to look more closely at how your child learns best, and to adapt to that as much as possible.

If we have to remember a story for a school discussion, we may remember it much better if you act it out together with figures on a table, or if you make drawings of key scenes.

Look into it, try to find your way ahead, and communicate with teachers to find the best way for your child to learn and retain knowledge.

MISTAKES

As mentioned in the section about handwriting, there can be a great deal of perfectionism and therefore also frustration when mistakes are made. In terms of handwriting, a letter not being shaped perfectly can either cause a meltdown or will prompt us to erase and redo it until it is perfect. Scott, an autistic man, wrote to me about this:

> "Attempting to write poetry or sign checks ended with numerous pages being torn out and thrown away. Journals were left unused because the writing process took so much effort the substance of what was being written was forgotten." (Scott, personal communication)

If a mistake is made in a report and marked in red by the teacher, the reaction can be very dramatic, because to us, that red mark does not mean we made a mistake; it means we are stupid, and that everything about that report is bad and wrong. This is black and white thinking; it is lack of nuance. Making mistakes makes us feel as if it is the end of the world, and that nothing can ever fix it again, because we cannot take back that mistake.

What we need is to develop a positive view of mistakes. This takes a very long time to learn, but in my view, it is also one of the most important skills for us to learn because everyone will keep making mistakes all through their lives. There is always going to be one more.

Again, take up the wonderful world of roleplaying games and Social Stories. Create stories and games exploring someone making a mistake and learning from it. Talk to your child about how, sometimes, people make the same mistake many times before they have learned to correct it, but it does not matter how long it takes as long as you try your best.

Encourage the view that it is okay to be wrong, and it is smart to admit when you are wrong and be open to changing opinions based on facts and evidence: that this does not make you stupid, but, in fact, shows how smart and mature you are. Do not expect this to take hold quickly. It goes against our natural inclinations. But after some years, you may have helped your child to develop the skill to accept and even appreciate mistakes as learning experiences.

TIME-SCALE

The last point I want to make about homework is one about time-scale. When a teacher sets an assignment, they usually have an idea of how long this task is supposed to take. But your child, with their way of thinking, their perfectionism and their exhaustion after a school day, will be likely to spend much more time and energy on each task than intended by the teacher.

Talk to your child's teachers about setting a time-scale on each homework assignment: an estimate of how long they think it should take. It could be 30 minutes or two hours, but if the teacher takes two seconds to write that on the piece of paper they hand to your child, then you know that the assignment is not supposed to take half the night. Your child should not be struggling to get through homework assignments for three times as long as was intended. They need and deserve time off.

With a time estimate on each assignment, you know to tell your child: "You will be spending 30 minutes on this one, and if you are not done, that is okay."

They will have put in the time and energy, but they also still need time to relax and recover from the day because the complete and utter exhaustion from a school day is something most autistic people have experienced. A young woman with Asperger's, Signe, wrote to me about the exhaustion from school:

> "I never did my homework. I did only what I had to hand in, but only just. I sat down for an hour or two and typed away, not even bothering to spell-check. I did just fine in school anyway. I was so tired and run down after school that I would just sit in the living room and watch TV until my parents came home, and then I would go to my room and read." (Signe, personal communication)

◇ Section 2 ◇

Relationships

Siblings

See also:
◇ Empathy and Sympathy ◇
◇ Theory of Mind and Social Reasoning ◇
◇ Social "Languages" ◇

I do not have any siblings myself, but many of us do, and many professionals make a point of speaking to both the autistic children and allistic siblings. This chapter is based on information and ideas I have gathered through such channels. Because more trouble tends to occur when there are both autistic and allistic siblings, rather than when both/all children either are or are not autistic, I will be discussing the former situation in this chapter. So, when one child is autistic and another is not, what should you be aware of as a parent?

THE SAFEST CHILD THAT IS NOT ME

Other children are strange and confusing, and it is hard to get to know them. But a sibling is someone you watch every day as you both grow up. Therefore, a sibling will, for better or worse, be the child you know the best, after yourself. For an autistic child, that almost by default means it is the safest child to be around, simply because they know what to expect. Use this familiarity to create positive bonds between them. The relationship may depend on the age gap and who is older. With a big age gap, the older siblings can help to create a positive social environment. And the older the other children are, the more likely the young autistic child will see them as role models and feel safe to ask them for help. With a smaller age gap, the allistic child might become a defender and a spokesperson, or the autistic child could become a teacher's assistant with you being the lead teacher, and in either case, give both children a sense of safety and pride about being kind and supportive to one another. I know, easier said than done.

WHY DO THEY NOT UNDERSTAND ME?

With siblings it can always go two ways. The autistic child may wonder why their sibling does not understand their quirks or why they do not share their interests. Likewise, the allistic child may wonder why their sibling does not understand why certain things are annoying or important. And this confusion becomes greater because it is a sibling; it is a child that is so close, who has seen and shared many experiences, but who may still not understand very important things about the other.

Autistic children can feel very confused about why their allistic sibling does not want to play the same games—and again, vice versa. Why do you, or do you not, think that this LEGO® collection is the greatest thing in the world!? So as a parent, you want to encourage them to play together, and help them find ways to do this. You also want to encourage and help them to understand each other where this is difficult.

THE SPECIAL NEEDS TAKING PRIORITY

This is, once again, cause for confusion. Especially for the allistic child. Why does my sibling get to eat certain things or, as might more often be the case, get to not eat certain things? Why does their sound sensitivity have to affect my play?

Of course, as the children get older, many things become easier to understand. But one effect of focusing on the needs of the autistic child is that this child will not get to see you, in an obvious, tangible way, taking their allistic sibling's needs into account to the same degree that their own needs are taken into account, and because of this they may have a harder time understanding their sibling's needs.

Because of that, and for exercises in empathy, make sure that you talk to the children (both together and separately) about how to make their sibling's life easier, and congratulate them and compliment them when they do things for each other and for you. This also encourages a value system where other people's needs are prioritized, for both autistic and allistic children.

Another possible problem is that the neurotypical child can feel overlooked. If your autistic child has special teachers or assistants, or possibly a nanny/carer with knowledge of autism, your other child can get a feeling of "Why does he/she have an adult to themselves?", especially if that child is still very young.

Take care to arrange for alone-time with both parents for both children to make sure they each are getting personal attention at some point. It may seem obvious when it is put in writing, but the more troubled one child is, the more the other can often be left to themselves, and while most find coping skills, it is still something to keep in mind.

DIFFERENT RULES FOR DIFFERENT CHILDREN

There are usually different rules because of age. An older child is allowed to do different things than a younger one. But when the differences are because of something other than age, they are a little harder to explain and understand. And for young children, it is very hard to understand what it means that your sibling is autistic and needs different things than you do.

Fortunately, children are not prejudiced by nature, so an honest explanation, simplified to be age appropriate, is a good place to start. They do, however, have a sense of justice, which means that reasoning must be fair. If you are explaining something to the autistic child, it also has to follow autism-logic, which can be trickier.

The really tricky part is making the explanation age appropriate. For example, it is very hard to explain to a young child that their sibling eats the same thing for dinner every night because you are doing your best to prevent a meltdown caused by sensory overload. Depending on the sibling's age, you could try things like: "He/she is the sort of person who prefers to eat the same thing for dinner every day" or "...gets scared when things are different than usual."

Especially when dealing with young children, I recommend avoiding language that makes it seem like an illness or disorder. This can cause several problems not only in communication but also in how they view each other and themselves. You do not want one sibling to view the other as inferior, wrong or defective, but rather as different. You especially do not want the autistic child to view themselves as ill or wrong. Therefore, try to find language that is neutral. Hence "the sort of person who...," as, sometimes, children have an easier time understanding that.

This leads to another, slightly connected issue, which is a tendency to praise different children for different things, and in different amounts for the same things. This is not necessarily a bad thing, but when it is audible to both children, make sure they both get the high-five for having put on their pyjamas correctly. Just as importantly, make sure that both high-fives are equally enthusiastic and honest. It may be that the younger allistic child has done it perfectly every evening for the last year or two and that this is the first time your autistic child did it correctly/without complaint/the first time you said to/whatever else has been the problem—but if both children can hear and/or see the first high-five and "Good job!", they both get one. Again, it might seem obvious in writing, but in practice, it can easily be forgotten.

YOU EMBARRASS ME BUT I STILL DEFEND YOU

Children who have autistic siblings can have very ambivalent feelings towards them. On the one hand, they can be embarrassed when their sibling does something in public or in front of friends that is not quite "normal." It is frustrating to have a sibling who has been making the same noise, or playing the same song, for the last hour, no matter how much you know they are fascinated by it. On the other hand, they are also often the first to defend their siblings when others stare or ridicule.

It is okay to feel embarrassed. It is not the reaction one wishes they had, but it is there, and it is how they feel. That is okay. It is not okay to voice it in a patronizing manner or in public, but it is okay to feel it. It is also okay to feel frustrated. It is okay to feel angry at times.

If you see them react to someone staring or perhaps even saying something back, for example: "It's rude to stare at someone else like that. He/she can't help being who he/she is," make sure you encourage this and reinforce standing up for their sibling as a good thing and make sure they know that defending them makes them a good sister or brother. Acknowledge their feelings, and encourage them to defend their sibling, no matter who is older and who is younger.

FLAWS ARE EASY TO SEE

Anyone can probably name something annoying about a family member they live with. Flaws or frustrating characteristics are easy to notice and easy to remember. And when children go to school and generally into the world, there will be no shortage of people who can tell them what they are not good at.

So, an exercise, once again in empathy but also in bonding, is talking about the things each child is good at and likes to do. One might really like to sing or to memorize lyrics, one might like a certain computer game. One could be really good at spelling or coming up with stories, one might be good at imitating voices or drawing.

Encourage the children to notice what their sibling likes to do and what they are good at and encourage them to complement each other from time to time (the autistic child might need to know exactly how often to do so, or need extra prompting, but may also overdo it—either way, it is something to work on and with).

Friends

See also:
◇ Social "Languages" ◇
◇ Theory of Mind and Social Reasoning ◇
◇ Aging, Growing Up and Puberty ◇
◇ Harmful Strategies and Risky Behaviour ◇

One of the most common concerns I hear from parents is that they feel their child has very few friends and therefore must be lonely. Most autistic people do feel lonely sometimes, but it is not necessarily because they lack friends. It is more often because we have a very hard time finding people who truly understand us. This means that our best chance at not feeling lonely is to find other autistic people who have similar traits and interests. That said, most of us like to have a few friends, no matter if they are autistic or not. For most, one really good friend is all we need. This is especially true in childhood.

For many, the number of friends they can cope with will slightly increase as they get older. One friend might take all one's energy as a child, two or three is plenty during the teenage years, and so on.

FINDING FRIENDS

We can have real trouble finding friends, both as children and throughout the rest of our lives. There can be several reasons but, mostly, it boils down to social awkwardness, difficulties reading others and naivety. We are unsure of how to initiate contact, how to maintain it and how to get positive attention from peers. Even when we get positive attention, we can be remarkably bad at spotting the signs of friendship from other children, as explained by Liane Holliday Willey:

> Looking far over my shoulder, I can call to mind people who must have been interested in friendship. I can see a boy I knew as if it was yesterday. I can remember his face and the expressions he made as we talked. Today if he looked at me like he did then, I believe I would have seen the kindness and gentleness that was his. I never did much with this boy when I had the chance. I missed his offer of friendship. I would not miss that offer if it were made today. His face would make sense to me today. (Willey 1999, pp.61–62)

We are also bad at spotting when peers are using us or when they might be "playing nice" in order to lead us into traps of bullying. In short, we are bad at spotting predators.

At this point, I should like to refer back to the Social "Languages" chapter. If you haven't read that section, this would be a good time to do so. It should give you an understanding of why I think it is important to learn social skills, should we wish to, even if we cannot all learn these skills perfectly. Any amount of skill in communicating who you are is better than none. Unfortunately, young allistic kids are not likely to all go out and learn how to communicate with us, so as children, making up for the difficulties on both sides of the communicative differences is left up to us. Of course, sometimes we meet people who are genuine and wonderful and who will do their part. People like these can become lifelong friends.

KEEPING FRIENDS

For autistic people, friendships take place under different terms than they do for others. First, we tend to have few but very important, close friends, rather than many. This means that when we reach out to a friend, we often do not understand how or why they can be busy, and we may get jealous of their other friends if we feel neglected. These are difficult emotions to deal with when you are a child, and it is equally difficult to understand why our friend does not feel the same way.

We are exceptionally loyal friends, generally speaking, and often consider someone a close personal friend, even if we have grown apart. If they have ever been important to us, they will remain important for a very long time, even after an active friendship has ended.

And when it comes to how active a friendship is, this is where misunderstandings can easily occur. Because for us, it might very well be enough to spend one day a month with our best friend. We can also be on the other extreme, where we have to see them every day. So, our friends can feel either neglected and not feel that the friendship is that close or important because we spend so little time cultivating and maintaining it, or they can feel absolutely suffocated by our attention.

As a parent, you can help to step in and guide us. If we are suffocating someone, try to make rules (and explain them) about how many times per week it is okay to call the same person, and how many times a month there should be playdates. If we are letting a potentially close friend become neglected, you can try to encourage us to call them or to socialize with them at school in some way.

Some will need relatively little guidance and others will need every minute detail explained and rehearsed. Social profiles and learning styles can be very different. Just be sure that you keep in mind the reason you are teaching and guiding your child. It should never be about making them "normal," but rather it should be about giving them ways to adapt to the world while retaining who they are in order to give them the best foundation for being happy.

The transition from child to teenager is where many problems in keeping friends can occur because the allistic peers will change their interests and behavior much earlier than we do. This is also when many experience bullying, where we previously were more accepted. Jimmi wrote to me that:

> "When I was little I did not want a lot of friends. It was the games that mattered. I had several friends to meet for

> playdates and my social needs were met completely. Later, in school, I made one really good friend, whom I saw more than the others. He also really liked hanging out with me. It was a great time. But in the teenage years it all started to change. Suddenly my really good friend also wanted to be with the 'in' crowd. Our close friendship was waning. It was also in the teenage years that the bullying began and went on. I was bullied throughout my teenage years. I was an outsider and a loner, who missed having friends in general and felt very lonely. Today, as an adult, I have a few really good friends, and many acquaintances." (Jimmi, personal communication)

I included the last part of his email because I feel that it is important to add that though the teenage years can be so horribly lonely for many of us, we do find friendships again, either in other autistic people or simply once we find allistic people who are less judgmental. Our friends—the ones that last—are people who accept who we are, our difficulties and qualities, who take our social skills and sensory sensitivities into account, and who view us as equals.

Such people can be hard to find, both as a child and as an adult, but they are the only kind worth finding. My advice to both parents and children is that they are also worth looking for.

NUMBER OF FRIENDS

When it comes to the number of friends we have and the importance of that number, autistic people generally fall into two categories, each at an extreme. Many are supremely happy with having one or two close friends, and, sometimes, two can even be too many. At the other extreme are those for whom it is vitally important to have a great number of friends.

Usually, for those who want many friends, it is not deep personal friendships they are looking for. They want to be popular and well-liked, and they, as many allistic people do, measure their popularity by their number of friends. These children will often speak of any person who is kind to them as a friend, and when they engage in social media, they will want everyone to accept friend requests—sometimes regardless of whether they know the person or not.

Again, some guidance can be useful, but usually in the form of building a sense of identity and self-worth. This does not mean that they want these friends because they feel badly about themselves, but merely that ensuring a good self-worth and a well-defined sense of identity will help to shield these children against being hurt socially. These children are more likely to succumb to peer pressure, and if bullied, especially in a group setting, will respond very strongly and emotionally.

The children who are overwhelmed by even a very low number of friends should be supported in keeping the friends they want to keep. You should also be ready to have a conversation or 30 if a friend moves away, becomes disinterested or if the children grow apart, and so on.

For these children, their friends are people they feel safe with, and they will usually be more socially reserved. They are not likely to call anyone new a friend because it takes a while to earn such a title. They are less likely to care what others think and therefore less likely to succumb to peer pressure. This, unfortunately, also means they are quite likely to be bullied at some point during their school years.

But to these children, it is the opinions of their one or two friends that matter, and the few friends are more important to them than any number of acquaintances or online friends.

A DIFFERENT KIND OF FRIENDSHIP

One of the things that both parents and children have to accept is that, for the most part, the friendships we make exist under a different set of circumstances to those between allistic people.

Our ways of spending time together are often more structured or have a more specific purpose. Where others might just "meet up for coffee," we will instead meet to watch a certain television series or movie together, or as in my case, meet up and play a tabletop roleplaying game where we already know which game it is, which characters are played and who is going to be there.

Even if your child goes on to just "meet up for coffee" or "meet up for dinner," it is likely to be a very small number of people that they can do this with whilst feeling comfortable, or reasonably so.

We tend to be in the extremes when it comes to how often we see and speak to our friends, either relatively rarely or every day. Some are perfectly content with not meeting people very often at all, and perhaps not even speaking very often. We are very different when it comes to this. A young woman with Asperger's wrote to me about the friendships she maintains and best feels she can cope with:

> "I found out that I'm much better at maintaining friendships with boys [than with girls]. It's also mostly over Skype, with two or three of them, only meeting physically once in a while. It doesn't seem to be a problem that you don't speak to them for half or whole years, and then write once in a while when something happens within a common interest. It probably helps that most of them are also on the spectrum, or very well could be.
>
> They aren't very close friendships in the typical sense, but it does prevent me from losing myself in the process. It seems to work because I can contact others when I actually have the energy to talk." (Signe, personal communication)

When it comes to people we know well, our friends can become an anchor when we are in situations that make us anxious. For example, if we go to a movie in a new theater, a concert or perhaps a private party, the friend we have with us is the safety net. They will be the person we mostly speak to, and they will be the person we arrive and leave with—especially if it is a party.

ALONE IS NOT LONELY

This leads me to a question I am often asked by parents. Should you be worried if your child only has one friend? If they do not go out much? If they spend hours upon hours alone in their room?

No!

To an autistic child, alone does not mean lonely. They are poles apart in this respect. As I talk about in the chapter "My Room," we relish solitude, and we need it. Some a lot more than others.

Quite often, a parent will have a very different view of their child's social needs and situation than does the child. Children and teenagers alike can be quite happy spending eight hours a day alone, while their parents are worried sick about their child's loneliness. (One thing to note here is that this amount of alone-time is usually desired during years where attending school is required. This means their social capacity is taken up by interactions in their learning environment.) Again, look at your child's profile and listen to what they say. Your child is very unlikely to tell you that they feel happy with their friends and their lives if they are actually miserable and lonely. The vast majority of autistic people wouldn't even think of telling that lie, and for a further immense number it would be very obvious if they tried. Every autistic person needs some amount of alone-time to function well. Some more, some less, but we all need it. And that is okay. We are not sad when we are alone. We are at peace, we are happy.

NEED FOR PLAYDATES

As with the number of friends, parents often have a greater need for playdates than their autistic children do. One playdate per month might be more than enough for your child, so do not worry about arranging several a week. It is unnecessary and stressful for your child, and it will not cause them to learn social skills any faster; they have to do this at their own pace and desire.

However, as with anything else, I must stress that we are all different, but that we tend to fall at the extremes. Our need, desire, and energy for playdates can vary greatly. Some will be very socially motivated and be less drained by it, while others are either less socially motivated—and thus, less inclined to want many friends and/or playdates—or they can be drained of energy very quickly from social activity, and despite social motivation may need you as parents to help make sure they are not overloaded and eventually run into burnout by it.

> "It's hard to get friends so I appreciate the ones I have. But it's easy getting playdates. I'm tired after having friends over but I can go to school the day after. I like having three or four playdates a week, sometimes five. Sometimes it's the same friend and sometimes different ones." (Anonymous, personal communication)

Many others I have spoken to have explained, especially as they grow slightly older, that they did need their parents to set a limit to how many playdates a week, or even to make sure there were none on weekdays. Many of us tend to be tired the day after socializing, and so playdates during weekdays can, for some, take away the energy they need for school.

WHO TO INVITE

You cannot choose your child's friends for them. They know who they like and who they do not, and trying to match them with children you think would be good for them is not going to work. Playdates should be with the children that your child already likes or is interested in knowing and playing with. We are people who can be very picky about our social interactions, and we can react with a lot of anxiety when someone chooses a play-partner or attempts to form a friendship on our behalf.

Also keep in mind that a child whom you perceive to be very sweet and fun may have done or said something when you were not around which has shaped our opinion of them, and we may not be able to communicate this to you.

ACTIVITY

For the most part, the children your child will want to play with will be the ones with similar interests or who have the patience to at least put up with a certain game for some amount of time. This means that the activities that will be engaged in during playdates will for the most part be the things your child already likes to do.

Do not try to force a new game onto your child because they are playing within a social context rather than alone, because if they are not prepared, they will not understand why you are doing this, and they may very easily become frustrated.

It is not really that hard though, because the children that are friends with your child already know who they are and what they like, usually from school or another such environment, so they can somewhat easily adapt to the situation. Very often, the children's games will consist of being together doing an activity they would normally do on their own, or sharing the same physical space to play alongside each other, such as LEGO® or computer games.

This can and will probably be the solution far into the teen years, and sometimes even as adults. Luckily, playing computer and console games is no longer seen as a strange hobby; it is something almost everyone does to some extent.

TIMEFRAME FOR PLAYDATES

Consider how much energy your child spends on being social and how they feel in general at the time. Are they extra stressed out, for example, because of a new teacher, the color of the neighbor's fence having been changed or a family birthday that is coming up?

Consider also which days you invite children over. On school days, most autistic children and adolescents are so exhausted they can hardly see straight, so those are bad days to add something extra to their schedule. So, keep it to weekends unless you have a fair idea that your child can cope, and keep the playdate to an amount of time that allows your child to recharge in time for the week ahead. Also, for us, simply having a timeframe can be important. Signe, who has Asperger's, wrote to me about her playdates:

> "I was known for wanting to control the games when I was little. When I had a playdate, it had to happen according to my head. I got angry if it did not happen the way I thought it should, or I did not know what to do if my friend got me to do something else. I also wanted to play the same thing over and over. I don't remember how long my playdates lasted. But I remember that I always used to think 'When are they going home?' or 'When is it okay for me to leave?' Not because I did not want to be there, but it would have given me a sense of calm if there had been a set time for the playdate to end." (Signe, personal communication)

If the child knows their own social needs and energy quite well and is able to know when they do not have the energy to have a friend over, they may then have problems with how to communicate that to the friend who asks. They may be too honest, hurting their friend's feelings. On the other hand, they may also feel pressure to make their friend happy and say yes, even though they know they will be too tired the next day. However, there is a great way around this, as Andie explains:

> "When I was a kid, mom and I had this agreement when I called home to hear if I could play with people. If I wanted to play, I'd say 'Mom, can I play with xx today?' and if I didn't want to, I'd say 'Mom, I cannot play with xx today, can I?' and she'd make up an excuse on my behalf for why I couldn't play that day." (Andie, personal communication)

Autistic people can be very good at this sort of "code speak" if they are given the option and taught how to use the codes. In this situation, Andie would be able to avoid a playdate that she was not feeling up to, without hurting the friend's feelings, and leaving open the option to play another day soon.

Guests

See also:
◇ **Friends** ◇
◇ **My Room** ◇
◇ **Vacations** ◇

The assumption in this chapter is that the guests in question are yours. Playdates are covered in in the previous chapter about friends.

Keep in mind, as always, that not everything will apply to your child, and that if they require less support to cope with the new situations it's important not to overdo it.

INFORM YOUR GUESTS

This is rule no. 1. All guests that your child will be interacting with should be informed either of the diagnosis or of anything different they are likely to encounter. The latter is most important. They do not necessarily need to know "My child has autism/is autistic," but they do need to know "My child cannot participate in conversation while eating, because it is overwhelming for them." Do not turn it into a problem, and do not expose your child to the conversation you have with your guests—do it over the phone, or at least away from the child. Making a remark in front of them about a certain way that they are different can make them feel anxious. They are not necessarily embarrassed, but probably just feeling pressure from attention being on them in a way that they do not know how to react to.

If something unexpected happens, try to take it in your stride and communicate your way through the situation. As always, the most important rule is to stay calm. Do not panic if your guests say or do the wrong thing with your child, even if your child acts out. Breathe, calm down, and handle the situation like you would any other day. And of course, do not blame the child or the guests for things going wrong. Your child reacts as well as they are capable of, and your guests cannot be expected to remember everything about your child's profile. Even if they also have an autistic child or family member, their profile is likely different. This means you are the intermediary, translating for each party and helping to avoid any conflict.

MANNERS AND SOCIAL EXPECTATIONS

Be aware that when you have guests over, you may have a subconsciously increased need for behavioral perfection. It can also be entirely conscious, of course, but either way, this should be given up as it will not do any good. Since you will be more anxious, this is likely to make your child more anxious. You will have a greater risk of reacting negatively towards something your child does that you wouldn't normally react to, for instance. Allistic children may handle this okay, but an autistic child is less likely to. In general, it is best not to correct your child while guests are there, if it can be avoided. There are several reasons for this. One is that your child is already processing more information than usual because of more people being present. This means they cannot cope very well with the added pressure of being corrected, as they are already stressed. Another reason is that children can feel very embarrassed if their behavior is corrected in front of other people—not to mention the guests may feel the same—and may become highly anxious as a result. They may even begin to develop anxiety around guests and the idea of people being invited to their home because there is this negativity associated with it.

Instead, keep things as close to normal as you can, because this will meet your child's need for sameness, and thereby you will avoid unnecessary anxiety on their part. You should not expect your child to engage in small talk because while non-autistic children can feel uncomfortable and bored with talking to adults about school or friends, an autistic child may feel downright frightened at the concept. Your child might, however, be thrilled to lecture about their special interest, and if they play a musical instrument or write stories, they may (or may not) be keen on showing their skills to anyone who will listen, and sometimes also those who will not. But small talk is not likely within their skillset.

DINING RITUAL CHANGES

There are several aspects to this part of having guests. There are new people at the dining table and family members do not necessarily sit where they usually do, but if you can, make sure they do. And most importantly, do not change where your child sits.

The fact alone that there are new people around the dining table can cause all sorts of confusion and tension in your child. This may further influence their eating habits. If it does, there is a reason, so try not to push them. Rather, if possible, have them sit alone to eat if this makes them more comfortable than being at the table. If nothing makes them comfortable, try to accommodate them and create positive experiences with the guests through appealing to their special interest or giving them access to pleasant sensory experiences. They may have a blanket of a particular fabric, a stress ball or if necessary, a music player with a headset. If possible, communicate to your guests beforehand if such things will be at the dining table to avoid confusion or them making comments while there.

Also, when there are guests for dinner, there is conversation between courses for the adults to engage in. For the child, it will often feel like a void and, normally, we would fill that void with something: either go and play until the next course is on the table or sit with the tablet/phone or help in the kitchen, whatever your child normally does if there are two or more courses. Try to keep this ritual for them even if it may seem rude to your guests. Try to explain to them that your child has certain rituals that make them feel happy and safe, and that any change in their day-to-day life is very upsetting. You may tell them the specific diagnosis or not. What is important is that your guests know not to scold your child for these behaviors, even when you are visiting them, and if they can, not to mention it at all. The inactivity between courses can be especially grueling if we know there is dessert, because many kids like dessert, and most kids will bounce around asking when dessert will be served. When you have an autistic child, you have the perfect solution to this: when your child wants to know, simply give them a timeframe to work within. You can either say a certain time, or if your child deals well with the concept, say that it will be before a certain time, giving yourself ample room to not stress. For example, if dinner starts at 6pm, you can tell your child: "Dessert will be served before 9pm." The timeframe should be one that your child can work with and should take their age and emotional maturity into account. Waiting is something we all have to learn.

Lastly, the earlier your child can be excused from the dinner table, the better. The exception is if your child is happily giving lectures about everything they know, of course. But, generally speaking, it can be an uncomfortable situation for us, and more so the younger we are, and the sooner we can escape into our room and play or read or engage in an interest, the better. You can also put a timeframe on this, if your child responds well to this coping mechanism.

As with everything else, note that for some autistic children, the opposite is true. As one autistic woman wrote to me:

> "I always liked listening to the grown-ups talk. They actually had reasonable conversations about interesting things that I could learn from! Unlike other children." (Charlotte, personal communication)

FAMILIARITY WITH GUESTS

Our stress and anxiety responses to guests can be vastly different, depending on whether we know the people in question. When we meet new people, we first have to figure a lot of things out about them. Unlike allistic people, we have a hard time generalizing our experiences from one "type" of person to another similar "type" of person. At the other extreme, there can be a tendency to over-generalize.

When an allistic person meets, for example, a priest, they will use their former experiences and connotations with priests to form a quick idea of who they are dealing with. They might think of traits like god-fearing, good, helpful, calm, trustworthy, knowledgeable, a confidante, and so on.

The picture they form in their mind of the concept "priest" is then evolved into the picture of "this priest," as they get to know him better. So, while there is an element of prejudice, it is a useful form of it, in most cases. Autistic people, however, can have a hard time associating general traits with concepts, and transferring them to new people who fit said concepts. This means that when we meet a new person, we start with a blank slate and have to fit in every trait as we go along. This means it takes longer for us to trust people and feel comfortable around them. Once we know someone, there is much less anxiety associated with being around them because the slate has been filled in, and we know who we are dealing with.

So, while you have to prepare us extensively to meet someone new, you can give shorter notice (though preferably still a few days) if we are meeting with people who are familiar to us.

WHEN TO HAVE PEOPLE OVER

When making plans for people to visit, consider how much energy your child has to cope with the extra social expectations and the knowledge that other people are in the house. This really goes for all guests and also for playdates. If your child is already worn out from the day at school, it might not be good to stress them further. If they have school or an event the day after, then social activity today may take away the energy they need for tomorrow.

When I speak to other autistic people about guests, they mostly say one of two things. The slightly rarer statement will be that they really like having guests over, but that it is draining, so it must be planned around in order to avoid being completely run down for several days after. The more typical statement will be some version of this:

> "Home is my sanctuary. It is where I relax, recharge and retreat after a day of people and the outside world. Therefore, I don't particularly enjoy guests. Even when I finally leave the draining dinner of questions and small talk, I still can't really relax. Other people at my house, even in another room, is not optimal for my much-needed alone-time." (Ellen, personal communication)

This, of course, results in even more alone-time being needed than would otherwise have been the case.

FAMILY HOLIDAYS

Naturally, the advice about food also applies here. If there is a traditional dish associated with a particular holiday, for example, Easter or Christmas, that makes your child ill, either to eat or to even smell, please do not force the child to deal with it. Tough love is not an approach that will produce any desired results.

Give the child the option to go and be alone, whether you are at home or at a family member's house. This is a fantastic coping mechanism, as it provides an escape route. Most children will actually be able to cope with more social activity when they know that they can leave at any time.

Be aware that your expectations of social activity may be higher. Your family members may also expect more of your child during these holidays. Try to decrease these expectations, and if you feel that your family members are hurt by your child not participating more, remind them that your child is doing as well as they can.

One more issue that can arise for Christmas and birthdays is giving and receiving gifts and having polite responses to getting unwanted items. We all sometimes will experience getting a gift that we did not really want, so try to discuss in advance and create Social Stories and roleplaying games about giving and receiving gifts, exploring the emotions felt by the parties involved, depending on the reaction they get from each other.

Also, simple rules-of-life can work really well: "If you do not say 'thank you,' people will be hurt and sad and think you are ungrateful, and they will not want to get you something next year."

You should be aware, however, that your child will then expect everyone to follow this rule, every time, and get annoyed and confused if they do not. If the rule applies to them, it applies to all.

One thing to note is that your child may be prone to getting ill after larger breaks in routine, such as guests, parties and family holidays. This is usually a stress reaction and can sometimes be solved or lessened in severity by giving the child time off (either in the form of removing demands or by being very structured, depending on your child's profile). As an adult, I will usually schedule a day or two following vacations to de-stress and allow myself a smoother transition back into daily life. If I do not take this time, I see the consequences of that a few weeks later. As a child, the consequences would come much sooner and usually take the form of illness or nosebleeds.

Bullying and Peer Pressure

See also:
◇ **Friends** ◇
◇ **Social Media** ◇
◇ **Harmful Strategies and Risky Behaviour** ◇

Bullying is not just an issue that most autistic people meet at some point in their lives. In most of our childhoods and youths, it is a fact of life. What most people fail to understand is that the others do not have to hit you to hurt you. In some cases, they will physically hurt you, but in many others, it is done with words and social exclusion. Much could be written about different forms of bullying and the effects they can have. I will focus on some types of bullying and effects that are more common for autistic children, and the ways the child or teenager might think.

It is also worth noting that while this is rarer, autistic children who are socially motivated and really want to fit in with their peers may join in with bullying another child in the effort to be liked by others. They may or may not realize that they are being cruel. They may think they are just going along with the social culture and not realize that they are actually bullying someone.

WHO CAN BULLY, AND HOW?

We used to define bullying mostly as a physical act between peers, but these days we acknowledge different forms of bullying, and also that the bully is not necessarily a peer of the victim. I would like to form a picture that can help you to see how a person can be victimized and by whom.

Bullying can, of course, take a physical form which, at least for the most part, can be seen by bystanders and may leave physical marks on the body. Another form of bullying is social exclusion. It may sound relatively harmless: "The other kids just do not want to play with you..." But there is a difference between other children not taking an interest, and actively excluding you. The exclusion is very obvious, and it is made to be obvious to the victim by the bully or—as is more often the case—bullies. It is intended to be hurtful, and even though some autistic children do not respond to this type of bullying many others do and are very hurt by this. Emotional bullying is very often connected to both the former types mentioned. This takes the form of ridicule and humiliation. Most often, this is done by a group, and the feeling of humiliation intensifies the more public the bullying is, especially when no one takes your side or attempts to protect you.

So, who can bully your child? You might think it is probably just other kids you have to worry about. I am very sorry to tell you that while your child's peers will make up the vast majority of probable bullies, there are examples of teachers and other adults in similar positions of authority participating actively in bullying. This can take the form of humiliating the child in front of peers or making statements privately to the child that are cruel and intended to cause anxiety.

There can be a degree of bullying from family members. In addition to the aforementioned types of bullying, family members can torment a child by dismissing their handicaps and/or diagnoses, actively provoking, for example, sensory sensitivities—sometimes in the genuine belief that the child is making it up and wanting them to admit it or stop being "difficult," other times in the erroneous belief that this will de-sensitize the child to the sensory experience.

A somewhat newer form of bullying, which has arisen with the advent of the internet, chat rooms, forums, social media and with children having their own phones, is cyber-bullying. What makes this exceptionally damaging for the victim is that there is no escape. With other forms of bullying you have a break once you are home. School might be hell, but at least you can leave.

When your tormenters are with you constantly—via text, social media, online computer and console games—you have no place to run or hide. This means you are constantly confronted with your tormenters, and even if you block them, they can make new accounts to continue their harassment if they are persistent enough. Cyber-bullying can take several forms. It can be done directly, by sending harmful messages, posting status updates or comments that are intended to hurt, but it can also be done in other, less direct ways, for example, by impersonating someone—which is more easily done than you might imagine—or by doc-dropping/doxing someone. Doc-dropping is when someone posts personal information such as telephone numbers, addresses or other means of directly contacting their target. Most often, several pieces of information are put out simultaneously. Videos intended to embarrass can be also taken and posted on various sites or apps.

There are, unfortunately, quite a lot of suicides directly connected with this form of bullying, which makes it all the more important to teach your child to protect themselves online. Make sure they know: Do not give out personal information, only give your username to close friends, block people who harass you and do this quickly. Take screenshots of abusive or harassing messages, including the usernames of those who wrote it, save these and file them. Keep evidence in case you need it later.

Keep in mind that if an adult is involved, it is called cyber-harassment or cyber-stalking, and different laws will apply. You can research this online, and I recommend starting with sites like www.stopbullying.gov/cyberbullying/what-is-it.

Sidenote to this section: Because many autistic children and teenagers are more easily manipulated than others, they may be manipulated into taking revealing photos or videos and be victims of a phenomenon called revenge porn. This is a heavy and complicated topic, and I recommend you do research online, check legislation in your country, and speak to your child about the risks associated with other people possessing images of you. Do this a few years before the age at which you might worry something could happen. Your child will need extended processing time, they will have many questions, and they will have to be prepared for what to do and what not to do if the situation does arise.

If anyone does manipulate your child before the age of 18, it will fall under child pornography laws. In this case, be aware that depending on the country you live in, your child can potentially be charged with the crime as well, having taken pictures of themselves and possessing them.

PEER PRESSURE

Peer pressure is common, but when it comes to autistic people, there can be different concerns than with neurotypical people.

For those who have a higher social motivation and with a tendency to worry about others' opinions, there can be a very high sensitivity to peer pressure. Furthermore, they can be sensitive to what they perceive to be the expectations of others. In cases like that, the child can bend to perceived peer pressure, not just explicit peer pressure.

This is often connected to the desire to fit in with peers and there can be a vulnerability, both to being pressured into going along with things they may not feel good about, but also to the social grief of having tried to appease others and those attempts not resulting in feeling more accepted or included.

Others may not respond to peer pressure at all or even notice that it is happening. Not responding to peer pressure can be connected to one's sense of justice, in that if the child thinks it is wrong to do something and is not swayed easily by others' opinions, they will not be convinced to do it. A strong sense of identity can be helpful in resisting peer pressure as well. Likewise, a child who is not socially motivated is less likely to cave to peer pressure. However, be mindful that such children can still be manipulated by others in different ways.

Not reacting to peer pressure can cause conflicts, as other children may react poorly to someone who does not follow the wishes of the group. Your child may need your support, such as reiterating to them that following their sense of identity or justice is a good thing to do.

If peer pressure rises to the level of bullying, the school may need to get involved, or parents may need to come together to help solve the issue.

EMOTIONS AND THEIR CONSEQUENCES

As you will know from the chapter "Amygdala and Emotions," we tend to feel in extremes, so if we feel humiliated or afraid, we may feel it to such a degree that we cannot calm ourselves down, much less think rationally. It also means that once our buttons have been pushed, other children will see it, because many of us do not have the capability to hide it so as to protect ourselves. This means that we are a perfect target for bullies. For many autistic children, our buttons are worn on our sleeves, we are socially naive, and we can react strongly to being teased and bullied. This is everything a bully wants in a victim.

Due to the emotional reactions we have, our way of thinking can quickly be affected and, combined with the child's profile, this can decide any number of more or less permanent ways of viewing the world and others in it.

There are two basic reactions to being bullied: externalizing and internalizing. Neither of these patterns of reaction are more or less "self-absorbed" or "ego-centric" than the other. Everyone has one or the other to some extent (or some combination of both); autistic people simply have more difficulty regulating emotions, and therefore whichever reaction they have comes out stronger and more dramatically.

EXTERNALIZATION

As humans we have three basic, instinctual reactions to threats: fight, flight or freeze. Externalizers tend to react with fight, yet instead of hurting the people who they feel threatened by, they may very well break or throw objects. This might happen when rage or anger, often propelled mostly by fear, can no longer be contained within them, and instincts take over. Rationality is long gone, and the best thing is to remove the threat. However, be cautious of leaving the child alone as their lashing out can overlap with internalization. Reacting outwardly can become about hurting oneself as well. For example, they may slam their hand or head on something, sometimes to the degree of actually causing damage to themselves, especially since the child may not have the reflex to stop when something hurts.

The externalization can also evolve into direct attacks on the people who are hurting them. This may happen especially if the child has concluded that the bullies are predators, monsters or enemies, rather than "people," but also if they feel they have no other option, for example if they are cornered.

The lack of trust which, initially, is reserved for the bullies or "enemies" can also expand into becoming a general state of emotion for the child. They will react to several groups then: the "primary bullies" or "active bullies," the "secondary bullies," who are the active followers who participate but do not initiate, the "passive followers," who watch, maybe laugh a little, but do not directly participate in the bullying, and lastly the "silent majority," the people who watch or know about the bullying, but do nothing to stop it.

In the case of this last group, I am reminded of the famous quote attributed to Edmund Burke: "The only thing necessary for the triumph of evil is for good men to do nothing." A child who feels wronged by those who do nothing to stop bullying may develop intense negative emotions towards them. They may have a hard time building positive relationships with these individuals in the future, even if the situation changes.

Teachers can fall into these categories, as well. If the child feels that the teachers know and do nothing, or that perhaps they even participate, this can cause a great distrust not only of peers, but also of authority figures.

This lack of trust can have a domino effect, expanding suddenly to include almost everyone as the child has learned that "no one cares." These children can thus have or develop a tendency toward being distrustful, toward angry and violent reactions, and sometimes toward arrogance, a type of thinking where it is assumed with certainty that everyone else is wrong.

For these children, taking the Emotional Toolbox and Cat-kit (see the Empathy and Sympathy chapter) into use can have great benefit. An Emotional Toolbox, as developed by Tony Attwood, is a visual overview of strategies which may be helpful when experiencing different emotions. There are resources online, for example at Milton-keynes.gov.uk or spectrumtherapy.com.au.

Note that the outward reaction displayed by some autistic children and teenagers is not simply anger, but an agitated, externalized depression. This term is applied to depressions which are expressed through anger, violence, consciously behaving badly and possibly engaging with a harmful social crowd. It is a relatively new term, and research is still being done. In this case, fixing the behavior of anger and violence will not solve the problem. You will need to look into the causes of the depression. Again, I recommend the Emotional Toolbox and Cat-kit.

INTERNALIZATION

The child who internalizes has a high risk of unfortunate reactions to traumatic life events, whether these occur in childhood or later. With the "internalizer," we need to watch out for depression, anxiety, problems with self-esteem and self-worth, eating disorders, self-harm and potential suicide attempts.

Most people think of depression and any of these other problems as things that affect teenagers and adults, so I want to make this very clear: Young children can experience clinical depression too. I personally had my first major depression when I was seven years old. It lasted for three years and included serious considerations of suicide for almost the entire duration. It was brought on by bullying, and I only improved once my environment changed such that I was no longer around the bullies. In my case, it required changing schools entirely.

Depression, anxiety and suicidal thoughts can occur from a very young age, and I am in no doubt that others, younger than me, have had the same thoughts. The younger your child is when first experiencing these thoughts and feelings, the more difficult it is, as they might think, as I did, that it is normal to think and feel this way. And it does indeed become normal after a while. So they might not, as I did not, tell anyone about their thoughts and feelings.

So, what are the inner thoughts of an internalizer? "Why me? It is always me. There is something wrong with me, or they would also pick on others. I am alone. No one will help me. They always want to hurt me."

These children might experience a sort of paranoia of peers and may assume that peers always have bad intent towards them.

The low self-esteem and self-worth will in some cases be noticeable, but in others, they may know enough about acting/masking to be able to pretend to be okay, so as to not worry a parent—especially if they feel the parent already has enough to deal with. The same goes for depression and suicidal thoughts.

Self-harm and eating disorders usually do not begin until the teen years, but it is possible to see them in children as well. However, remember that an eating disorder in a child is not necessarily a result of bullying, but can be a sign of other things; see the discussion about eating disorders in the chapter "Food and Dinnertime."

Note that self-harming behavior, eating disorders or other such extremes should be taken very seriously and you should contact a specialized professional.

THOUGHTS THAT CAN DETER SUICIDE ATTEMPTS

If your child suffers from suicidal thoughts, it is important that they have other thoughts to keep them from actually attempting suicide. Whether the suicidal thoughts are constant or come only during "depression attacks" (like anxiety attacks, a fairly sudden and intense experience which passes in either minutes, hours or a day's time), there needs to be something that blocks the child from acting on the thought.

This is one of the areas in which conventional methods may not work, and you need to consider your child's profile. Once again, I suggest consulting with a specialized professional.

Some of the thought categories that work for people on the spectrum are:

The effects on family/animals of my being gone

Here it is thoughts like "Who will feed the dog?" or "My parents will be very sad."

Missing an exciting experience

Perhaps a new movie is coming out, or a trip to a place that has to do with a special interest. It can be things that seem completely trivial but having some experience ahead that is interesting and exciting can be the thought that leads to the "Not today" conclusion.

Not solving the problem

This one can be understood in two ways. If the child is working on a project of some kind, there can be a desire to finish it. The other is this: "Suicide does not solve the problem of how I ended up feeling this way. The problem wins if I die." This is a more complex thought that requires the child to have a certain profile. Many others will think of suicide as the solution to the problem, rather than something to overcome, so this way of thinking may not work, though it does for some.

Fear of not succeeding

Strangely, the prospect of failing to die may be seen by the individual as something shameful. It links to fear of pain and fear of being found out as reasons not to act on suicidal thoughts. It would be hard to raise these reasons with your child directly, but they may come to them on their own. Of course, if you have concerns that your child may be experiencing suicidal feelings then dangerous items such as firearms should be removed from the home to create as safe an environment as possible.

The special interest

It can function as a distraction at times where you would not think anything could. If at all possible, I would keep something that concerns the child's special interest near or on their person at all times. Something they can see, touch, smell or hear. If they love Batman, it can be a figurine in their pocket which they can grab and hold. If they love a certain song or movie, make sure they have it on a device with them, along with headphones. Make sure it is charged—they may forget that detail, especially when in a depression. Try your best to schedule things that have to do with the interest at regular intervals, and make sure the child knows when it is.

Social Media

See also:
◇ **Profiles** ◇
◇ **Friends** ◇
◇ **Bullying and Peer Pressure** ◇

Social media plays a large role in our daily lives. This includes how we communicate with the people we know and care about, how many young people get their news, and how they educate themselves on general trends in society.

Social media, both browser- and app-based, tends to move faster among younger generations, and even for neurotypical children, there are both positive and negative aspects to it. For autistic children these problems and benefits, while in essence the same, can be exacerbated.

DANGERS OF SOCIAL MEDIA

Social media is designed to catch and keep your attention. This is because most, if not all, popular social media makes its money from ads and data, and these only make money if people are spending their time on social media. What this means is that it will keep trying to hold your attention by feeding you posts or ads or information which will keep you scrolling. Naturally, the same thing is happening when your child uses social media.

It can almost lead to a social media addiction, in which the person feels unable to stop even though hours have passed. They may feel obsessed with reading every post about a certain topic, or simply lose track of time.

One result of social media platforms being built this way is that if you are interested in certain topics, it will keep feeding you posts about that topic and ones expressing the types of viewpoints that keep you reading and scrolling. This means that you will be unlikely to get exposed to different viewpoints unless you look for them explicitly, and that the viewpoints you are exposed to can become more and more extreme, or fringe. This means, unfortunately, that social media can be a recruitment ground for communities that can have harmful ideas, just as they can the opposite. There are communities that are hateful in one way or another, or promote self-harm, idealize people who have committed horrible crimes, and more.

This means your child can be at risk of becoming radicalized by communities such as these without you ever seeing it happening. It will be important that you speak to your child about their viewpoints on many topics, and that you pay attention if you hear them say something that suggests they are being drawn into communities with extreme views. Remember that the algorithms may have prevented them from seeing balanced viewpoints on these topics for a while.

For autistic people, who can have a tendency to see the world in absolutes, or who may not understand how social media works and how this can result in being manipulated, there may be an increased vulnerability to this manipulation. If they have been exposed to communities which promote eating disorders, for example, their ideas of beauty or health may have veered very far from the norm. However, some autistic people are also very prone to seeking out information about such ideas and may be very good at fact-checking. This would be a protective factor for that person, and it can become an interest to help educate others who have been misled. (Note that this can lead to conflicts online, but that it may also be an indication that the person could become an educator or consultant in that field later in life.)

Another result may be that the person becomes afraid to speak their minds. They see how upset and cruel people can be in comments online, and so they may not post anything themselves, ever. They may also think that people react that way in "real life," and become very quiet and rarely voice their opinions or thoughts about anything. On the other hand, they may also be led to believe that this is how people discuss things and take the tone they see online with them into face-to-face conversations, not realizing how hurtful that may be. Personally, I see the former happen much more often than the latter.

Using social media can also have a strange numbing effect on one's brain. An autistic woman wrote to me that:

> "I also find that my brain feels really frayed and scattered after I have been using social media. It is like the opposite of meditation and makes everything I try to do afterwards a lot harder, because it is harder to focus and I have a million little stupid thought fragments in my head." (Charlotte, personal communication)

EASIER ACCESS TO FRIENDS

One of the largest benefits to social media is the easy access to communication with people in one's social circle, or with like-minded interests. It also makes it relatively easy to find friends or contacts all around the world.

There is, of course, the speed of communication that is available, but this is the norm in our time. For autistic people, social media removes a lot of the stress and exhaustion from socializing. Reading facial mimicry, body language and vocal intonation is not required in text, and while there can still be the need to read the "tone" of a message, it is far more acceptable to be a little slower to respond, which can provide time to think or to ask for help to understand possible meanings if in doubt. It can also give you the opportunity to consider the content of what you send to others, as Andie explains:

> "Communities over Discord have given me access to friends in other countries who share interests with me. I prefer text-based social media, because I can re-read and edit messages before I send them, which means there are fewer misunderstandings than in real life." (Andie, personal communication)

On the other hand, waiting for a response can be difficult. It may be hard for a child to understand why their friend is not responding at the same pace as they themselves are, why they may not be available to chat at the same time. It can also be difficult to have that expectation put on them by their friends. If they are tired from socializing, get distracted by a different interest or must be away for another reason, the expectation to be always present and quick to respond can be very overwhelming. For that reason, it may be very helpful for your child to talk about how to quickly communicate that they have to leave the conversation for either a short or longer timeframe. This can be things like writing "brb" for "be right back" if they are only gone for a few minutes, but it can also be to let their friends know that there is a family dinner at a certain time, which means they will have to put their phone away or walk away from the computer. There will be relevant short forms for such communications, however, as these change somewhat rapidly, those included here may be outdated. However, it could be things like "ttyl" for "talk to you later," or in computer games, writing "afk" is used to say "away from keyboard."

Social media is also a way to share created content with friends and like-minded individuals. This could be YouTube videos, TikToks, memes or much else. In fact, the options will likely become more plentiful within a relatively short timeframe and any list I could make would be quickly outdated.

Creating and sharing content can be a great way of bonding with others and sharing interests, and it can bring a lot of joy. Of course, anything that exists on the internet can also be a target for criticism, especially from strangers, but also from potential school bullies, should they find it. Therefore, it can be especially important to notice the positive comments, and as a parent, it will be important to support what your child is creating and to help them cope with any negative comments that come their way. Another option is, of course, to keep created content private such that it is only shared with the select few for whom it is intended. However, there is a culture of making public content, and so you cannot expect that your child will not be interested in that too.

◇ Section 3 ◇

Spaces and Events

My Room

See also:
◇ **Profiles** ◇
◇ **Stimming** ◇
◇ **Guests** ◇

As a child, even as early as age six or seven, my room was my favorite place in the world. I did not have a lock on the door yet, but I would have a hook on the door to lock it before I turned 10. Knowing that it was my room and no one could come in unless I wanted them to was my greatest relief.

My room was almost always incredibly messy. Not dirty, per se, just messy. There were LEGO® and dinosaur toys all over the floor. I wanted it that way. I liked it.

I spent most of my time in there, and I was never unhappy there. In my room, with my toys, I could enter a different world that no one could touch. No one could take it away. As soon as I got my first stereo, the toys were replaced and music now allowed me a new and different fictional and emotional world to enter. I never wanted to leave. I still do not.

Any parent of a non-autistic child would have probably been concerned. When a child of 10 has only one or two friends and spends as much time as they are allowed to in solitude in their room, most parents get concerned.

But I think my mother realized that solitude was preferable to me than being forced to socialize. She realized that my room was my sanctuary. My haven.

Solitude is so very valuable to autistic people. We need it like we need food and sleep. It provides the emotional and mental restorative, the peace, which allows us to continue facing the world. Think of it as meditation. Time spent in solitude, engaged in a special interest is great, but it is also the knowledge that you will not be interrupted that makes the difference.

UNDERSTANDING THE LANGUAGE AND RULES

My room. It is a room that is mine. Property. Territory. Mine. This is important because of the way we understand language vs the way others/you do. When you say "Your room" to a child, you probably mean "Your room is in my house, which means there are certain rules that apply that you do not get to control, because I am still the boss. We call it your room because that is what people call it, but it is actually ultimately under my control because it is part of my house," or to paraphrase, "It is my house and you are given use of that room for as long as you live here."

We can compare it to governments and plots of land within them. You buy land, and that makes it yours, but it still ultimately belongs to the country it is in, and if you break the laws of the country—whether you do it on your land or not—you are in trouble. Likewise, if I do not follow my parents' rules that apply to my room, I am in trouble. Many autistic people do not understand this in the same way that you do. Our understanding can be more akin to: "It is my room. If it is not mine, do not call it mine. And if you want to make agreements about which laws apply in my room, they had better be reasonable, and you have to provide the reason along with the rule/law."

You will have an even worse time having an autistic child in your house if they do not have a room to call theirs, because we need to have a place we can go and know that we are alone and will not be disturbed.

So, to make things work, it is all about making sensible rules for that room, for example:

"You have to clean your room so it does not get too dirty, because otherwise little bugs start taking over and they will get into the rest of the house/apartment even though I clean it. I do not want these bugs because..."

"You have to tidy your room every week/day/whenever because this makes it easier and faster to clean. It also means you always know where your things are—they will not get lost. It means you will not be as overwhelmed by having to tidy because there will not be quite as much mess."

YOUR GUESTS AND MY ROOM

One rule most parents want to enforce is that the room must be tidy when guests come over. This is not an easy rule to try to convince an autistic person of, and here is why:

If they are your guests, they do not need to see and especially do not need to enter my room. I do not want them there. If they have kids, and those kids are given access to my room, they will want to play with my toys. I do not want them to. It is no use tidying before they show up anyway, because if they get access to my toys, they will make a mess. In short, my room is not yours to show off to your friends, even if I like them, and it is my choice if I let people in there. It is my choice if others get to touch my stuff.

Unfortunately, I cannot recommend a way for you to get your way on this point because it is not logical. If you want it your way, try rewards. Autistic logic dictates you are wrong on this matter, and so you will have to make it worth their while to tidy and show their room to your guests. However, if your child feels very private about their room, it can feel like a violation to be "forced" to show it to people they do not feel quite as comfortable with. When it comes to trust, like so much else, we tend to fall in extremes, and so your child may have an incredibly easy time trusting new people, but more likely, it will take them a long time to develop trust. It can be months or even years. So please take this into account when considering who you are asking your child to let into their safe haven.

DESIGN AND DECOR

Most parents will want a happy room for their child. One with happy items and colors; one that is bright and "gives energy." However, autistic children often have a very firm idea of how they want their room to be, regardless of what their parents might think.

One person I know had lots of pillows with different colors on each side of them, because that way she could turn them over to whichever pattern of colors was pleasing to her on that day, all depending on her mood. This might be something most parents would find fun or, at the very least, acceptable.

I always wanted my curtains closed because when they are open, I feel exposed and anxious. I also wanted dark colors because they soothe me. This is not something all parents are likely to understand, and certainly not something I could explain at age 10. I just knew what I wanted.

I am naturally not suggesting you follow every whim your child has, and especially not if their requests change often. I can imagine how hard work it would be to paint their walls a new color every week. However, I am saying that although our tastes can be very unconventional and sometimes very precise in detail, there is usually a reason behind our wishes for how we want our rooms to look, and if you can find some way to accommodate our wishes, you might very well have fulfilled a deep emotional need, even though we do not have the words to tell you this.

WHAT IT MEANS TO ME

As I mentioned, my room was always my favorite place to be. It is for many, if not most, autistic children. It provides us with solitude and downtime. This is where we can breathe. It is the place where all expectations from other people, all the pressures we are constantly under, disappear. I am not sure if I can truly explain the peace and relief of being alone in your room.

Perhaps you can compare it to a primal human, alone, being chased by a predator of some kind—let's make it a lion—and finally, after a whole day of running and dodging attacks, this human finds a cave that the lion cannot enter. It is still outside, but at least it cannot come in.

This is the immensity of the relief that I, and so many others, feel when we come home from school and lock ourselves in our room. It is our safe haven, our stronghold. The only physical place where we feel truly free. Due to our strong attachment to this private space, there can also be a reluctance to let others come in and see it. As previously mentioned, it can almost feel like a violation because people get too close that way. A young autistic woman wrote to me that:

> "My room has always been a free space; a place I could be myself. That's why I have always been very worried of potential friends' reactions to my room, with it being so personal and private for me. Therefore, I also prefer meeting my friends at their place or other places, because then I have my private sphere at home, where I can unwind without any social demands." (Signe, personal communication)

If our special interest can also be indulged in within the confines of our room that only makes the relief and peace greater. Unfortunately, this has a side effect, because it means that many of us do not actually ever want to come back out. For most, it gets easier with age and maturity to control the urge to stay in our cave, and to go out and face responsibility, school, work and people. For others, it gets harder: usually due to bullying, anxiety, depression or simply a lack of confidence, which normally builds for years before we truly become hermits. However, this outcome is very rare for those who are diagnosed (or otherwise find out they are autistic) before adulthood and given the necessary support. This support will be different for each person, of course.

The key words there are "necessary support," as there can be quite a difference between the support we need and the "treatments" imposed on us by people who want to cure us.

LIFELONG NECESSITY

Many parents may want to try all sorts of things to get their child out of their rooms and have hopes that we will become "more social" with time and age.

To date I have never heard an autistic person say that they could live with another person without having a room to themselves without feeling much more stressed. It can be an office, a gaming room or a workshop. Usually, it has something to do with the special interest. But the room is there. It might be called something else, but it is a room that is only theirs, and which any partner does not simply enter without permission.

When your child is an adult and wants to move in with someone, they should probably make sure that the place they move to has enough space for "their room." Otherwise, it can be detrimental to their mental health and their relationship.

I experienced this problem myself when moving in with a boyfriend and having a shared office, thinking that as long as there was one more room aside from the bedroom and living room it would be fine, but realizing that, over a few months, I became much more tense and less socially inclined because the lack of a private room and alone-time was stressing me. The solution of being home alone whenever he was out helped to some degree but it is far from optimal. The need for "my room" has not disappeared or diminished for any autistic adult I have ever met. This, incidentally, does not diminish our love for the people around us, which is important to remember. It is equally as important to teach us to communicate this fact to future partners, because being social and meeting social expectations is exhausting for us no matter how much we love and adore the people we are social with, and the more our needs for a safe haven and alone-time are met, the more energy we will have to meet expectations and communicate in general.

HOW YOU CAN HELP

Your child's room should be their place where they are safe and happy. It should allow, if possible, for their special interest to be engaged in, which will go a great way towards happiness within that space.

If there have to be rules regarding the room, the time spent in it, when to come out, and so on, make sure these have sensible reasons and that you explain the reasons so the child understands why they are in place. Autistic children are not likely to adhere to authority if said authority seems to them to be unreasonable and unfair.

It is my opinion that some rules should be in place. Things like a set bedtime on school nights, keeping a somewhat tidy and clean room (not "Keeping Up Appearances"-clean, just so it is not unhealthy), coming out for dinner, and so on, are all good things. But the "why" is very important to an autistic child (or an adult) so I would suggest it might be productive for parents to think about the "why" and communicate this clearly to the child.

Respect your child's door. If it is closed, you knock. It may seem a silly thing that a parent should knock before entering, but it serves several functions. First, it shows your child that you respect their privacy, which is incredibly important to them. Second, it gives them a moment to prepare themselves that something social is about to occur, which again, is incredibly important to them.

So please knock and respect their response when this is sensible. Wait for them to say "come in" or otherwise communicate that they are ready for you to enter because this will reinforce the respect for their privacy, autonomy and allow them that moment to mentally prepare for interaction. If there are siblings, make sure they know and understand this, and for peace in the house, it might be good to have similar practices with them. Make sure the room is never a punishment, as again, you want it to be a place of safety and happiness.

Public Places

See also:
◇ Sensory Sensitivities ◇
◇ Clothes, Shoes and Shopping ◇
◇ Guests ◇

It is quite impossible to stay out of the public space with the way society works today. At some point you have to deal with the world. Public places present two big, unique challenges: the amount of social and sensory chaos, and the judgments made by strangers. The latter of the two unfortunately does not really have a solution, and all you can do is try to learn to accept that people judge and that they can sometimes be very rude and disrespectful. This is very difficult, as strangers can remark on our behavior in public, especially if we move slowly. I have personally experienced a stranger, another customer, verbally assaulting me at a grocery store for not putting my groceries up on the register quickly enough, and physically beginning to throw my groceries up there. Such experiences can greatly heighten our stress for hours or even days, and in cases where we are treated very badly can contribute to complex post-traumatic stress disorder (PTSD) or anxiety disorders.

What we can do to make it easier for ourselves includes learning and developing coping mechanisms to help deal with the sensory aspects of being in public spaces.

THE SENSORY EXPERIENCE

As with almost everything else concerning autism, one of the elements to consider is the sensory one. The stress created by sound from many sources at once makes it difficult to be in an area with lots of people. Because people talk. A lot.

For you, this sound probably for the most part becomes background noise. But for us, it is a buzzing in our heads that distorts other sounds and makes it difficult to focus on what you are saying, or what we are supposed to be doing. Likewise, the many different and sometimes very sudden noises from machines, vehicles, and so on mean that we can reach auditory overload very quickly. Of course, different people experience it differently, but this seems, from my experience, to be somewhat generally applicable. Suffice to say, it is uncomfortable.

Moving on to sight, there are colors and patterns we do not expect, and many different ones at the same time. There may be sparkling or shiny objects which can be distracting, or they can feel disorienting or painful to look at. This is frustrating and, while this is all background for you, it is assaulting our senses, making it difficult to focus on the things we know we are expected to focus on, and the things we, ourselves, would rather be focusing on.

To cope with the sensory experience of being out in public, many autistic people have developed ways of either blocking certain sensory inputs or decreasing the intensity of them. Those with sensitivity to light and/or eye contact may wear sunglasses. There are special colors of sunglasses that can be bought or custom-made if the light sensitivity has to do with a specific range of light. When it comes to decreasing the intensity of eye contact, the sunglasses (especially the very dark ones) can feel like a protective barrier between you and everyone else. This is not an option for everyone, but it does work for many. The colored lenses from the brand Irlen seem to be a very popular choice amongst autistic people, as several people have specifically recommended them to me. There may be many other options, however.

As for the overwhelming amount of sound, many have taken to the options of either noise-reducing headphones and/or playing music whenever in public. Ellen describes doing this to reduce anxiety as well as dealing with sensory sensitivities in public places:

> "I generally dislike being in public. I live in a big city, and with the noises being insane, I try to listen to music while I am out. It may sound weird to fight noise with more noise, but it works for me. It gives me something to concentrate on. If not, I get too caught up in everything that is going on. Strangers make me very uncomfortable. I freak out over what people might think of me and I know it's completely irrational, but I still do it." (Ellen, personal communication)

BASIC ANXIETY REACTION

This does not apply to all of us, but some autistic people, especially those who have experienced group bullying, may experience general anxiety from being in large crowds. It is not a phobia as such, but more a programmed anxiety that comes from expecting to get hurt. You do not know where the next jab is going to come from, but it might come and you are waiting for it.

A child or even adult might not realize where this feeling of anxiety comes from or why they are reacting that way, and because it is based on general anxiety, which does not necessarily present any outward symptoms—and it is not an anxiety attack—it will not be obvious to bystanders that the anxiety is even there.

This is especially important in cases of large crowds where the ability to move freely is hindered—as it can be in crowded school halls, for example—so it is best to try to avoid those sorts of situations if possible, also due to the resulting stress.

EXPECTATION TO BE SOCIABLE

There is also an expectation to be sociable in public. Not to engage in deep conversation or an exploration of the identity of others or ourselves, however. The social expectations of the public sphere are the small things. Do I look this person in the eye or not? How will they react? Do not bump into people and try to avoid them bumping into you. Most importantly, do not stand out. When someone does bump into you, do not react. Just keep walking. If it is your fault, remember to apologize quickly, but do not expect others to. Be ready to respond in a polite way if someone engages you in small talk, but do not engage anyone yourself (on the off chance you actually wanted to!) because you may misjudge your choice of conversationalist or not do it correctly, and they will be offended. This goes on and on, with these small, odd ways of social interaction that are expected yet unwanted, by us and allistic people alike (mostly in big cities), but nonetheless engaged in.

This is all annoying in different ways, depending on your age and social capacity. When you are a very young child, you have no coping mechanisms to deal with the sensory sensitivities you have. This means there is no additional energy or attention to deal with the social bits. So, when an elderly lady decides to ask you something or tell you something, it causes a meltdown rather than the cute smile she anticipated.

People stare at you when you read in public (perhaps just to see which book it is) or make comments about how rude it is to wear hoods or headphones inside. You, as parents, might very well be the target of comments about why your child is only wearing black clothes and never smiles—yet we hear it, too; we just cannot cope and do not know how to react.

As a teen, new problems begin as your peers begin to show one of two reactions to you. It might go in the "positive" way, and they begin making sexual comments and flirting with you. This is highly uncomfortable because for the most part, our emotional maturity is delayed such that at the time our peers begin doing this, we are not thinking in remotely the same direction. It is also uncomfortable because we simply do not understand what is going on and also often because the way allistic people flirt at this age is not amusing or attractive to many of us. And yes, this happens in public, too. It also happens in school. As does the opposite and negative reaction: They will make comments about looks, fashion, lack of experience, nerdiness, and so on. They make fun of you, torment and ridicule you, and again, we do not know what to do about this. We do not know how to react in the situation, and we do not know where to direct our emotional reaction to it once it is over. Having to consciously think through all the aspects of social interaction means the proper response is delayed, which can be a factor in being targeted by bullies or being victimized by strangers.

For the most part, the problem with public places is the combination of sensory sensitivities and the pure presence of so many people being in our personal sphere, bumping into us, sometimes making rude comments or staring.

The conclusion must therefore be that if you intend to take us to the Natural History Museum, do not do it on a Saturday. If we must go on a weekend, try making sure we are the first ones in, for example, so the trip will be as quiet as possible. Do not do it when the tourists are out and about. While we are still learning how it all works, processing new areas and buildings and learning the rules of public conduct, it is best not to simultaneously push the limits about crowds.

AMUSEMENT PARKS

These places have added layers to the sensory experience that most other places do not. The sounds we encounter of excited screams, many different pieces of music being played simultaneously, smells of different foods and people shoving things in our face, create a combination that is, for many of us, less exciting than it would be for allistic peers. To some autistic children, this is rather a description of pure hell.

When investigating whether this is fun for your child, find a smaller amusement park and go there on a weekday if at all possible. This is the same strategy as with museums, shopping trips, and so on. Start small and push slowly. If your child likes these things they will express this in one way or another, and if they hate it, you will likely know this too.

GROCERY STORES AND FOOD COURTS

Here the issues concerning public places and food-related sensory sensitivities combine. Even though the food is not right in front of us, we can still see it and smell it. In food courts there is an added problem in the pure number of people either using cutlery, messing with plastic and paper wrapping, chewing, talking, moving chairs and generally making lots of noise. In grocery stores, there may be aisles that are extra difficult for your child's senses, or certain holiday or seasonal periods where the decorations or seasonal items are overwhelming. Sounds and music in stores can also contribute to sensory overload.

Generally, the strategy should be to get in and out of such places in a fair hurry, but without stressing your child. This means giving them information about what is going to happen, and an estimate of how quickly it will be over. "We are going to buy these items, and if I suddenly remember something else, I will try my best to be quick about it. I expect it will take about half an hour."

(This advice will not suffice for a child with a higher need for detailed information, so if your child cannot cope with instructions like these, apply whichever version works for your child.)

Remember also that strategies which work perfectly fine most of the time may not work on a particular day, for example due to increased stress from other sources.

Some children like these environments, especially stores. There can be a fascination with the combination of colors on a certain aisle, or with memorizing prices of certain things. Your child might even enjoy trying to add up how much the total will be, by memory, as you are picking up items. If this is the case, allow them time to do this when possible, and in cases like adding up the total, help your child by making sure they have seen each item you put in the cart, and how many there are of them. If they get the correct total, they might well be happy, but if they are wrong they might feel bad. Encourage them to get it right, and help them to view mistakes as something positive that they can learn from.

TRANSPORTATION

A lot of people on the spectrum have trouble with using public transportation. Some because they find it to be a confusing mess; some because you are never able to predict with confidence if there will be delays, if you will be able to get the seat you feel comfortable in, how close you will have to stand to others and so on; and for yet others it is a matter of the sensory experiences and the fact that you know with almost complete certainty that it will be uncomfortable. Someone will either smell really bad or wear so much perfume that you feel you are choking, or someone might stare at you.

There are so many possible uncomfortable things about it. On top of this, if you have to remember schedules or you have a change that is difficult to make in time—possibly due to delays—or if you have a lot of changes to make, it can take up a lot of energy just to get where you are going.

I am lucky to live in a city where many things are reasonably close and our public transportation system can get you almost anywhere, but if I have to change more than twice, it gets to the point where even the idea of going on the trip is so stressful that I can have a hard time coping, and much more so if I am in a period of more depression or anxiety than normal.

If your child becomes stressed or anxious about using public transportation, see if it is possible for them to be driven instead and if it is not far, taxis could perhaps be considered. Even though it might seem a luxury, the reduction in stress can be quite significant. Instead of trying to predict changes in sensory environment and social environment and having to recall schedules for different modes of transportation, your child can have time off, sitting in one means of transportation, and therefore arriving at their destination with much more energy than they would otherwise.

Specific modes of transportation are also common special interests. Trains and airplanes are most common, in my experience. If your child has a special interest in, for example, trains, they may very much enjoy taking the train and will speak endlessly to both you and strangers about what type of train you are travelling on, giving details regarding its functionality and history. They may also want to take long trips that are unnecessary for your daily life, simply for the joy of being on the train. You may find that once they take public trains by themselves, they will want to go far and wide without remembering to tell you, precisely because they are so excited. For this reason, it may be a good idea to indulge this interest and to plan trips they want to take, so that you may be there to supervise them and make sure they get home safely.

Vacations

See also:
◇ Sensory Sensitivities ◇
◇ Food and Dinnertime ◇
◇ Public Places ◇

Everyone loves a good vacation: Taking some time off, seeing new places. Everyone, that is, except the unprepared autistic person. First of all, please make sure you have read the chapters "Public Places" and "Food and Dinnertime" because that content is very relevant here.

DO RESEARCH AND FIND PICTURES

Going to a new place can be really exciting and interesting and some people like not knowing what to expect. This cannot be said for autistic people. We like to know. We like to be prepared. How prepared we want to be depends on the individual, but some degree of knowing what we are getting into is always nice.

To satisfy this, and avoid any anxiety that might otherwise arise, you should prepare yourself to talk a lot about where you are going and what you will be doing there.

The first thing is to do some research about the place you are going. One idea is to ask your child to go online and find information and pictures to engage them in the process and planning. Find out which places you and your child want to see, sights and museums or whatever it might be. The more you can involve the child in doing this research, the more prepared they will be for the trip. If the place is of particular interest to the child, they may be very happy to play the tour guide once you are there. Again, take your child's profile, age and interests into account.

KEEP SOME STRUCTURE

When some people go on vacation, they prefer to change their daily routines around and adopt a more casual view of things. Depending on your child and their profile, they may be able to deal with this or they may not. The younger the child is, the less likely it is that they can, so I suggest keeping some of the daily structure even though all is not possible. Try to keep the morning routine as close to normal as you can giving your child the most positive and predictable beginning to their day possible. This will hopefully reduce stress and anxiety. Keep in mind that some autistic children would prefer that no changes ever occur. These children can be upset at not having to go to school, even if they are unhappy there. If your child needs a higher level of structure to their day, it is essential to keep this, even when on vacation.

PLAN FOR DIFFERENT SITUATIONS

Make sure there are plans that take different things into account: for example, if it rains one day, we will do this instead. Make Plans A, B and C, such that contingency plans are already available. For example, we are planning to sleep in on this day, but if we wake up early anyway, we can do this. Improvisation tends to not work out in the best way, so if all plans fail, attempting to return to normal daily life for the day may be the best course of action, depending on your child's profile. In general, planning and schedules are great—visual ones are best.

Make a plan for the day you are leaving. What are you going to do to get to the airport if you are going on a plane? What time does check-in start? Make sure you have time to walk around the airport—allow even more time if your child is interested in planes and airports.

Again, the need for planning may very well decrease with age and familiarity, and spontaneity can be introduced by the child.

Take their profile into account—how much planning do they want/need? How many times do they need to go through the plans? This all differs for each individual. I recommend erring on the side of overdoing it and being slightly annoying, rather than underestimating how anxious your child will get, at least the first time you go traveling. Once you have a better idea of how your child reacts in this type of situation, it will be easier to know what to do next time.

NEW SENSORY EXPERIENCES

Depending on how far away you are going, or what type of environment you are going to compared to where you live, more and more sensory experiences will change. The smells, colors, climate, and intensity of sunlight can all change dramatically. This means that your child will be adjusting to a whole new set of sensory inputs and experiences, and possible previously undiscovered sensitivities may now be "triggered" by stress and anxiety.

There will also be cases where the local cuisine is not appealing, even if the general experience of the new place is.

> "My family teased me a lot about wanting McDonalds in Spain as a kid. I have grown into rather diverse food habits, but I was not a child that wanted much diversity foodwise." (Andie, personal communication)

However, this can also come about due to overload. The child may actually be interested in trying the new food, but not have the capacity to cope with it because of all the other new sensory experiences and changes that are happening. This can result in the child wanting to stick with very simple, known foods, despite having expressed interest in trying new foods while the vacation was being discussed.

Some changes can be very positive, and some are unexpected, counterintuitive or do not make sense; for example, I may have to wear sunglasses during both summer and winter in Europe, but not always on other continents—the sunlight hurts my eyes less, as it is softer somehow.

If your child is used to feeling uncomfortably hot or cold, going somewhere with a colder or warmer climate, respectively, can also provide a sensory break in that regard and bring more energy or lessen stress.

Both personal experience and conversations with other autistic people indicate that we generally need a few days to adjust to a new place and to recover from travel. I always make sure that the first few days of a vacation are reserved for relaxing and calmly exploring the nearby area of the hotel. I also make sure that I have a few days off when I come home to readjust to everyday life. Both are crucial to coping with travel for me, and many others express the same need for time to adjust and readjust.

A part of this is also the packing and unpacking process, in which items are not where they are supposed to be and things can feel a bit chaotic. When packing, some will find it preferable to go about it slowly, over several days, and others will cope better with it all being done the evening prior to departing, having the weird empty shelves for only a night/morning. When coming back home, it is often best to unpack and get things back to where they are supposed to be quickly, rather than get stuck for several days in the process.

NEW SOCIAL CULTURES AND RULES

Other countries also have other social cultures and rules to follow. It is best to be prepared for these, so include them in your research. Certain hand gestures might mean other things than they do in your culture—a thumbs up can be rude, for example, or burping while eating can be considered the polite thing to do.

While such things can be confusing, they can also be fun and exciting, and present a chance to teach your child about how social norms can differ across the globe. It is a very good opportunity to expose your child to the fact that even allistic people can make social mistakes if they do not know the rules, but that we can all do our best to learn the rules and apply them, which results in fewer misunderstandings.

SPECIAL INTERESTS IN FOREIGN CULTURES

Autistic children develop special interests in all sorts of things, and one rather common interest is a different culture—usually one very different from their own and sometimes one that no longer exists. Some of the common ones are ancient Rome, Egypt, China and modern Japan. It can be almost anything. But whichever culture it is, such a special interest often develops into a great enthusiasm to travel to places that have to do with it and can provide the courage to go places and do things the child would normally be reluctant to do. It can stave off stress, exhaustion and anxiety to a great degree—we become so immersed in the interest and exploring it that it takes priority. The stress and/or exhaustion will catch up at some point, but you may be surprised at how long it takes.

Let your child explore but try to protect them a bit. They can become so immersed that they do not feel hunger or thirst, and it will be your problem to get them to sit down and eat. Of course, one great thing here is that you can test some things out concerning food, as traditional dishes from the culture of interest will perhaps have some draw.

School and Class

See also:
◇ Cognitive Abilities ◇
◇ Sensory Sensitivities ◇
◇ Social "Languages" ◇
◇ Friends ◇

While school parties and homework have their own chapters and many topics from other chapters are also relevant to this one, school and class as a general topic will be discussed here.

WHY IS SCHOOL SO STRESSFUL?

Just briefly, we need to cover what it is about school that causes so much stress. In essence, it is because it combines everything that is difficult already and adds the expectations of academic achievement to that. What does that mean? Well, consider the chapters on food, sensory sensitivities, homework, friends, public places and bullying, just to begin. There are aspects of all those things involved in going to school.

School is a place where you are not only expected to learn the subjects on your timetable, but to do so while you are socializing; coping with the sensory environment of the classroom, the playground, the other children and the hallways; keeping a good relationship with your teachers; and coping with any issues related to food in a highly social situation.

THE SENSORY STUFF

Just in general, schools and classrooms are filled with sensory impressions that can be triggering for sensory sensitivities. For many, the fluorescent lights can appear to be flickering, even to the point of being perceived as a strobe light. This is not only very disturbing for someone who is trying to focus in class, but can also cause headaches, dizziness or other physical reactions.

The many patterns on the walls, floors or people's clothing can also be a disturbing element. In the early classes, such as first or second grade, classrooms are more likely to be decorated by drawings made by the children, or colorful "fun" learning tools. For autistic children, these are likely to be irrelevant to their learning, and even possibly an annoyance to their ability to concentrate. The more colors, patterns and loose objects there are in a room, the more the child's brain is occupied with processing all of that.

Another issue are smells or scents. The teacher may wear a particular cologne or perfume; another child may have a particular food item in their lunch which triggers sensory sensitivities. This can make it difficult to focus and can also impair the child's ability to eat their own food at lunchtime. If we are feeling overwhelmed by the smell of something, our own appetite can completely disappear.

THE SOCIAL CLASS

No talk about school is complete without talking about the "social class." This is how I personally refer to it, but you will know it as "break time" or "recess."

Recess functions, for most children, as a short break where they get to move around, focus on something fun and give their minds some rest from learning. This is important because our brains are not made to be able to concentrate all day long. Generally, after 30–45 minutes, lapses in attention become much more frequent, and a short break will enable people to come back to the task and focus once again. So, recess is actually one of the most important aspects of the school day. Without it, your child would not learn anywhere near as much as they do.

However, this time for the brain to do something else, relax and then get ready to learn again, only works if the break actually allows for that relaxation to take place. Think of it like the breaks in between sets of repetitions in a workout—if you keep forcing that same muscle to keep working between sets, you are not able to complete the workout in the same way. You would exhaust the muscle if it was never given time to relax.

For an autistic child, recess is a confusing, overwhelming experience. The structure of the class is removed, and they are metaphorically thrown into the playground and the social class. This is a practical class with no teacher, no curriculum, no structure and no time to even adjust. You have to go into the "playground-classroom" and just do it. In many countries, recess will have varying lengths, with some breaks being five or ten minutes, and lunchbreak often being around 30 minutes. This means that the child with ASD has an hour of maths, then five minutes of "social class," then an hour of history, then five minutes of "social class," and so on.

Does this sound like a stressful day to you? I can tell you, without a doubt, that if you put any person, regardless of their neurology, on a timetable which interspersed learning periods with short additional learning periods but without telling them what they were supposed to learn or how, they would quickly become very stressed indeed. I personally suspect that this is one of the reasons many autistic children are diagnosed in early school or kindergarten years. They cope with this stressful weekly schedule for as long as they can, but eventually, they cannot manage any longer and symptoms of their mental health declining will become more apparent, along with their own soothing behaviors. They are not becoming more autistic, but they may need those soothing behaviors or the safety of their special interest much more.

> "As a child I used to hide in closets or lock myself in the bathrooms at school during classes, or even leave in the middle of class to go and hide. My parents spoke to my school about it, and because I was keeping up academically, they came to the agreement that it would be okay for me to leave and take a break whenever I needed to. This actually solved the problem, and made it much less frequent that I

> would leave class or avoid class. Somehow, knowing that I could get the break if I needed it, made me able to handle the situation much better. It also got much easier with age." (Andie, personal communication)

EXPECTATIONS AND RULES

Schools do expect children to follow certain rules and meet certain standards. There are rules for behavior, rules for when to be there—you can't skip or be late—and in some cases, rules for how to dress.

While autistic people often find rules comforting, it can be difficult if those rules are not communicated clearly, or if we feel that we are unable to live up to the expectations. Many autistic children feel that they are forced to make the choice between being at school on time and every day, and their own ability to function outside of school as well as learn in school. They may show up for all the classes but then not have the energy to complete their homework, or even to eat dinner at home. An autistic man whom I used to do presentations with would tell parents and professionals about how he would spend all his energy on being in school and behaving there. When he came home, every day after school, he would be so tired that he would fall asleep on the staircase leading up to his room, sleeping there for an hour or two before he had the energy to get up the stairs and go to bed.

This is to say there can be a cost to being rule-abiding. In many cases, it may be highly beneficial to make changes to the expectations the child has to meet, such that they can meet those expectations and feel good about themselves. This will benefit their long-term mental health, as well as their learning ability both in and outside of school.

Within the classroom, there may be rules for how to behave, which are usually in place to contribute to a quiet and calm classroom. However, it may be impossible for a child with ASD—or indeed with ADHD—to sit still if they are not allowed to doodle in their book, or fidget with an object such as a tangle. In such a case, it may be the best thing for the class as a whole to allow children to fidget, so long as it helps them to focus.

I recognize, certainly, that making the necessary accommodations available to children with ASD can be very challenging, especially if other children must understand why another child has special rules. However, as an advocate for autistic children, and for children's mental health, I have to encourage finding ways to do this. Doing what we can to improve their mental health early, such as by decreasing stress, will improve their lives for the rest of their lives. On the other hand, the earlier a child is stressed, and the more they are stressed, the worse their mental and physical health is likely to be for the rest of their lives. As such, I must underscore the importance of striving towards a more positive school and class experience for children and adolescents.

School Parties and Birthdays

See also:
◇ Profiles ◇
◇ Theory of Mind and Social Reasoning ◇
◇ Friends ◇

I realize that a parent hopes that their child will enjoy having many friends and having friends over for birthday parties. A parent might also very well hope that they can drop off their child at a classmate's birthday party knowing that when they come back to pick their child up, they will have had a good time.

None of this is to be expected when your child is autistic.

Let us assume that your child has not experienced bullying, and that their classmates are, if not understanding, then at least accepting of them and the differences in the way they behave. Their parents will not know the extent to which your child can or cannot participate, their eating habits, and so on. Your child's friend's parents do not know your child's autism. They may have some general knowledge of autism, and they might know something about your child, specifically, but they do not know it all, and you cannot prepare them properly though you can do your very best.

BIRTHDAY PARTY GAMES AND PLAY

Whether it is a competition of eating a string candy the fastest, balancing an egg on a spoon while racing, or jumping in a sack, kids make up games, and parents make up games that kids are all expected to participate in during these events. And often they are likely to either involve motor skills or food. Your child may be the very best at these (because by coincidence or planning, they cater to their specific skillset), or the very worst. It is likely to be the latter, due to the tendency for us to have difficulties in these very areas. This will perhaps sound petty and immature, but one less positive characteristic about autistic people is that if we understand the concepts of competition, winning and losing, we tend to really hate losing. Naturally, this does not apply to all of us. However, it is true for many.

Because of the way we understand language, we are very likely to be of the opinion (and very strongly so), that second place means you have also lost. Everything that is not winning is, by definition, losing. People who lose are often made fun of in contexts we have seen (even if we have not been victims of it), and so we do not want to be those people. In our minds, not being good at something, no matter how silly that something is, can seem like defeat. So many of us can react quite badly to not being good at things the very first time we try them. So, when we lose, we have to control ourselves tightly so as not to throw a fit, which is something we do not want to do because it is embarrassing. But having poor self-control, as children do, this can be extremely difficult, and if we succeed at all, we will have used up a lot of energy on this one task. This can all be avoided of course, if your child has learnt that not winning is okay, and that it is all in good fun. Some can learn this easily, and some never do, and even when they know it intellectually, the emotional reaction can still override the attempts to control behavior. If this is the case, try to find ways to avoid such games. (This would also include sports competitions and board games.)

A BULLY/TEASER PRESENT

One is much worse than the other, of course. There are gradients here, but the essence of the problem is the same. Someone is present whom you want to get away from, but you cannot get away. This is a situation which, as someone who has experienced bullying, I would try to avoid at all costs. I would rather not have had any birthday parties, and not attended anyone else's birthday party, if going meant I would be stuck in a situation with a bully. I already had to endure them at school, but outside? That was too much to ask.

Yet I was not given the option, due to the culture in my country, which dictates that you are supposed to invite everyone from your class (usually around 30–35 kids), or at least everyone of the same gender.

I would advise, on behalf of your child, to give them an option. If you know they are being bullied or teased, and that the offending child will be present, try to provide your child with a way out. If they have to go to the party, make sure they can call to be picked up with relatively short notice. If they are having the party, try to find some way to avoid the attendance of the offending child. For example, if the bully is of the opposite gender, can you then invite only the same gender? If the bully is the same gender, consider either only inviting the children that are your child's friends (regardless of school and grade), or not having a party at all.

Talk to your child about options and ask what they prefer. Try to have all options mapped out, including reasons why you have excluded other options. Explain it all in an age- and maturity-appropriate manner.

AND ALL THE USUAL SUSPECTS

As with everything else, the issues of sensory sensitivities and social exhaustion threaten to ruin it all. Try to take these into account, which, of course, is most easily done if you are hosting. But if your child is attending someone else's party, try contacting their parents and discuss with them what to do. Let them know what your main concerns are when it comes to, for example, sensory sensitivities—you do not have to talk about diagnoses or use the correct terms, you can use vaguer terms—and if you have time, offer assistance; "My child really dislikes strawberries, so if you plan to put those in the cake, would it be okay if I brought one without?" or "My child is allergic to strawberries, they make him/her very ill. If they are in the cake, would it be okay if..."

If your child's diagnosis is known by classmates or parents, or if you are comfortable with it, try to discuss the option of your child going to sit in a quiet room to have breaks from the social events.

Also, try to make sure your child can escape the party quickly if needed. Either give them the option to call for you or discuss with the hosting parents if they would be okay with you hanging out during the party or you could suggest that you assist if you think they will not be offended by the offer.

There are autistic children who have no issue with these situations. Again, it all depends on the profile of the child, and what they focus on in those situations. Signe, who has Asperger's, wrote a great example of this to me:

> "I always attended school parties and birthdays. I wanted to go to the school parties, because I like dancing to loud music. Unfortunately, I did not like the music they played, and when I suggested any of the metal or Celtic music I liked, I was ignored. Birthdays weren't awful, so far as I remember them. There was candy and soda (which I was very focused on as a child), and fun games, so I had fun even though I wasn't a part of the other children's groups." (Signe, personal communication)

Some children will focus so much on a certain aspect that it all becomes acceptable or even enjoyable. I, personally, relate to wanting to dance to loud music, and therefore being comfortable at school parties. It may also be that the child having a birthday party has a really nice dog, or they have a good swing in the yard. If this is what your child focuses on in those situations, do not ruin it by telling them they cannot play with the dog or whatever it is. Try bargaining with them and make deals with the other parents. They can play with the dog for 20 minutes, for example.

◇ Section 4 ◇

Interests

Hobbies and Extracurricular Activities

See also:
◇ Profiles ◇
◇ School and Class ◇
◇ Special Interests ◇

As with any other child, a certain number of hobbies or extracurricular activities can be very healthy, but with an autistic child, it might be hard to know which environments are productive and which can be problematic.

ENERGY

Always consider how much energy is left after school, and consider mental and physical energy separately from each other. They might be very tired mentally but can still benefit from some form of physical activity. It is also possible that your child's level of energy seems more than it is, simply because they are so excited about what they are going to do. In this case, it will most likely backfire in the evening or the following day.

This is a trial-and-error thing, I know, but it is worth trying to figure out.

WHAT SORT OF HOBBY?

What I want to do is different from what the other kids want to do. And on the off chance that my interest is considered normal, it will still be extreme in focus. I might love horses, but that does not mean I want to go riding twice a week; it means I want to go every day, and for much longer than other kids do. If my interest is dinosaurs, I will check out every book and watch every documentary, want to go to museums, and possibly even try to dig for fossils myself.

Your child is more likely than allistic children to have hobbies or special interests like chess, science, (rare or "cult") computer games, foreign languages, specific historical periods and the like. Even if others perceive it as odd, something about this subject or activity appeals to your child and the way they think. If you want to understand why this particular thing is so exciting for them, talk to them, ask them about it. They will be so happy to tell you why their hobby or interest is the best thing in the world. Other children and adults may not understand and may react negatively to it, and it is very important that you try to find the positive in their interests when others do not, in order to provide your child with social and emotional support. You may also have to explain to your child why other children are not as interested in the history of stamps as they are. It can be very confusing to someone so young why we are so different from everyone else, and why they don't like the things we like. Again, the differences in Theory of Mind skills could be at play.

TEAM SPORTS VS. SOLO SPORTS

Autistic children very rarely do well in certain types of team sports—yet there are exceptions!

Football, basketball, handball and that type of game is usually not the answer to getting your child some physical exercise. Generally speaking, sports that include balls, either throwing or kicking, are not our kinds of sports. And the teammates (and opponent teammates) will notice this quickly. Will Hadcroft wrote of his experience:

> I was frightened of the other boys, and this was very apparent to them. Tackling was a nightmare, and I let the ball go without much of a fight, to the fury of my fellow team members. (Hadcroft 2005, p.62)

Very often, good types of sports for us are things like martial arts (karate, kendo, thai chi, aikido, etc.), as there may well be some level of interest in the culture and history attached to this, or gymnastics, solo dancing and swimming. Less physical types of exercise can be just as useful in terms of meditative quality, for example, shooting, both guns and bows, because a great deal of concentration is required, and usually there is a somewhat long period between each shot. There is also a lot of focus on breathing, hand-eye coordination, and so on. All in all, it can be extremely mentally beneficial.

> "Training martial arts is very helpful in a number of ways. For one, the training is highly structured and you are told which technique to practice at what time. In most forms there are also clear rules for social interaction. In the Japanese martial art Aikido, for example, the hierarchy is clear from the belt colors and within belt colors experience decides the rank. If you are ever in doubt about anything social, the rule is to ask your senior in rank, and since they have more experience they will often know. If they do not know they will ask their senior and so on. There is only one master, and if there are any matters to be settled he or she will decide. Apart from the social rules being more clear than in other places, it is also a great way to have physical interaction with other people in a safe setting. And obviously you will learn ways to defend yourself which actually builds your self-esteem and thereby lowers your anxiety in situations of threat as you now know you have 'weapons' to defend yourself with should it become necessary. I have, personally, also found that having an interest in a particular martial art in common can bring about some good friendships over time—something which may not come easy to many of us." (Sif, personal communication)

NON-SPORT ACTIVITIES

Other activities that are highly beneficial and that we are likely to be or become good at are, for example, chess, art, languages and music. Again, a high level of concentration and forethought is required. In music, good fine motor skills are required to attain any professional skill level, but whether this is achieved or not, the playing of and interaction with music can in itself be beneficial.

Drama classes are also often a great joy. Naturally, it is mostly those who enjoy mimicking and mirroring behavior that are attracted to this activity. But drama classes and roleplaying are both great activities for teaching social skills and do so in a way that is fun and interesting. Do remember, however, that if your child tends to use masking behavior it can become a source of exhaustion for them. They may need you to let them know that their autistic behaviors do not need to be hidden away for them to be loved and accepted.

For most of us, LEGO® is an unparalleled joy for either a short or long period of time. There is something about building something, the planning, thinking out of details and creating a scene. Generally speaking, it is the building part that is important. Once we are done building, we do not tend to play so much afterwards, if at all. For others, of course, the story of a game will be the most important, but rarely will we want others to join.

When we get a little older—or when we are allowed computer access—we quickly find our way to games like Minecraft and the Sims. Once again, it is often the building part of the game we are interested in.

Whatever appeals to us, it does so for a reason and should not be downplayed as "just a hobby." For us, it is these "hobbies" that bring us joy, that allow us to think, build and create.

BENEFITS IN ADULTHOOD

Every hobby, interest or activity brings us something while we are engaged in it, but they also teach us things that can be brought into adulthood. For example, martial arts, meditative activities, swimming and dancing bring body awareness and a better ability to control our focus. They also give tools to control and regulate emotional reactions in situations where this is needed.

LEGO®, Minecraft, the Sims and the like allow us to fine-tune our attention to detail and indulge in it. This is a great skill for many jobs. Importantly, attention to detail is a trait that tends to be a double-edged sword, in that we may get distracted or upset by details no one else notices, or spend far more time on tasks than others, but it can also be used as a strength in certain tasks or jobs. Learning that traits can have positive and negative sides to them is also beneficial because it helps to teach us to think about the world in a more nuanced way.

All of this can be guided, and you have the opportunity to do this. This is to say, rather than thinking that our interests are silly or strange, think of how they help us to hone our skills for the future, and support them.

Special Interests

See also:
◇ Profiles ◇
◇ Hobbies and Extracurricular Activities ◇
◇ Self-Identity ◇

Other people have hobbies; autistic people have special interests. We can also have hobbies, but we tend to find certain things that are so interesting to us that the closest word to describing our interest would be "obsession."

They are interests that give us such joy that it can be hard to convince us to do anything else.

The first special interest can show itself at a very early age or not appear until late teens or early adulthood. Some people have only one for their whole lifetime. Others lose interest over time—anywhere from months to years to decades—and pick up a new one. Yet others seem to collect special interests. They rarely, if ever, lose an interest, but continue to gain them. This version can be very frustrating to the autistic person. They want to give time to all their interests, and having to prioritize between them can be difficult, emotionally. You want to give them all equal time, which is impossible, and you feel guilty about engaging in one interest because it means you are neglecting another.

It should be noted that, although this is rare, some do not have special interests at all.

GENDER DIFFERENCES

As with many other things, there is a tendency to have certain expressions of autism depending on gender, but, as always, you should never expect your child to follow any norm or prediction.

Stay open to any trait being expressed differently in your child. I refer you back to the "Profiles" chapter.

Generally speaking, people with the classic or "male" profile tend to have interests that are odd in focus as well as intensity. Examples could be air traffic, collecting batteries, or ancient Sumerian history—things that not too many people find fascinating.

People with the "female" profile tend to have interests that are more common in focus but obsessive in intensity. Boy bands, fashion, popular book series—what you will find is that while the interest is the same as that of allistic peers, the autistic person will know much more about the subject and spend much more time on it. Some professionals tend to divide more firmly into these profiles, but it should be noted that someone can have a profile that allows for both types of special interests. Special interests can also involve much more than collecting objects or knowledge. Sometimes they involve creating things: sculptures, paintings, drawings, music or things more uncommon.

ENJOYMENT

One of the important components of a special interest is the enjoyment we experience when engaging in it. It can be so all-encompassing that we forget everything else. All the bad experiences of our day, all negative thoughts and worries disappear, and we are inside the world of the special interest. Whether this is music, fiction or trains, the enjoyment is the same. In terms of enjoyment, the special interest is much more than a hobby. It is not something we just like to do; it is what makes life worth living. For this reason, taking away the special interest should never, and I do mean never, be used as punishment. Taking it away can trigger deep despair beyond what is healthy for a child to experience.

However, extended access to the special interest can be used as a reward system. If, for example, the child normally has access for two hours per day, a reward for completing homework might be an extra 15 or 30 minutes.

As a side note to this, if you see your child losing the enjoyment of their special interest, paired with any depressive symptom, if it no longer makes them happy and is not replaced by a new one, this should be cause for concern regarding their mental health, especially if depression is already a concern, or they have previously had suicidal thoughts.

Another quick note is that, occasionally, an autistic person can have a special interest which is not enjoyable to them, but which is still an obsession they cannot let go of. These types of interests are often subjects which are deeply interesting to the person, but not "fun" things and they are sometimes even disturbing to learn about. It could be world wars, certain types of diseases or even things like serial killers. In such cases, the person is still driven to learn about the topic as with any other special interest, but they may not get the sense of feeling happy or joyful, as the topic—despite it being fascinating—is not fun, *per se*. If your child has a special interest which they are driven towards but do not get enjoyment from, the special interest should be supplemented, when possible, with joyful activities. However, no matter how disturbing you may find the interest, do not attempt to take it away as this will not be helpful. Rather, do what you can to make activities available which will give access to relaxation and joy.

THOUGHT BLOCKER

When it comes to depression and anxiety, the special interest can be a very effective thought blocker. As previously mentioned, all negative thoughts can cease while engaged in the special interest, as we are so consumed with immersing ourselves in the interest and the joy it brings. In this sense, it can easily be used as a method to reduce anxiety and even to treat depression, although medication may be needed as well. Consider that it works by taking up all the space in our brains and focusing us completely. So, there is no room for thoughts concerning what happened in school, or the prospect of tomorrow being stressful. Everything is about the interest during the time we engage in it. Ellen describes how the television show Doctor Who did this for her:

> "Some might say that special interests are a hindrance, and though this can be true to some extent, they're mostly a positive thing. When I was depressed and bullied at school, the thought of coming home to watch Doctor Who helped me get through the day." (Ellen, personal communication)

ENERGIZER

While most other things drain our energy, the special interest is a great restorative. Aside from sleep and solitude, it can be the only way to truly recharge, and combined with solitude, it is incomparable. That said, it should be noted that some special interests can simultaneously drain energy as well. There is nothing to do about this, as we cannot force ourselves to have a different interest. I merely point it out to make parents aware of it.

If the interest is a computer game with a social aspect, for example, World of Warcraft, Conan, EverQuest, or another MMORPG (massively multiplayer online roleplaying game), the social aspect will be draining to some degree, just as computer games that have timers or require fast action in some way can also drain energy. The result is that while energy overall is still restored by engaging in the interest, it may not be as quick as with a previous interest, or it may restore energy in the form of making the child happy, but their social capacity has been completely filled. In such cases, I suggest consulting with a specialized professional to find solutions for optimal energy restoration during the time spent on the interest. This can include tools to make the social aspects of the game easier, giving the child reading material on the game (like stories about it if they like a roleplaying aspect of it, or blogs or videos with tips for improving game skills), or perhaps inspiring the child to write or make videos about what they have done and achieved in the game.

In the last instance, I strongly recommend these aren't posted online. Do not add yet another social component by posting blogs or videos, as the child is then likely to encounter criticism online, or "trolls," who are people who make a hobby of writing mean things to get responses from their victims. Your child can be very successful if they are good at making videos or streaming, but they need a certain degree of resilience to potential online bullying for this to be a good idea.

If your child writes a diary or story about their game, keep it amongst friends and family, and if they want you or others to read it, your commentary should be positive and encouraging at all times—remember, you are commenting on the topic that makes your child the happiest, and the happiness and enjoyment connected with this interest is vital for their mental health.

Your child can be extra vulnerable to criticism or negative statements about the topic of their interest; therefore, it is important to always keep a positive tone when discussing it.

SENSE OF IDENTITY

Your child's special interest can be a great part of their sense of identity. They may use terms in a similar way to adults describing themselves as doctors or teachers when asked who they are.

I am a roleplayer, for example, and I identify with this term just as much as with the term autistic. It is a part of what makes you who you are, and you feel like a part of a group just knowing that there are others with this same interest who identify in the same way. This also means that if there is a gap between two special interests, or even if one is gained and after some time the old one is lost, there can be an identity crisis. If I lost interest in roleplaying games, I could suddenly no longer say that I am a roleplayer, and this would mean there was a "gap" in the list of terms and adjectives that I use to describe myself.

It can therefore be a very good idea to have a talk about this if it is relevant. Talk about how the experience gained during the time engaging in an interest is still a part of who they are, and that even if there is no longer a simple term for it, they could call themselves a "former roleplayer" or a "former train enthusiast."

This means they can still appreciate having had this interest, and everything they learned from it.

Talk about how identity evolves as you grow older, and how this is good and normal and nothing to be concerned about.

POSSIBILITIES OF EMPLOYMENT

Some interests are exceptionally useful, both in terms of gaining skills and knowledge to ease your life, and of finding a job. Interests such as computer programming can lead to very well-paid jobs very early in life because the autistic person will often teach themselves the skill they are interested in from an early age. Other interests that can lead to employment in adulthood may include psychology, engineering, design and paleontology, and there are many more. Even an interest in seemingly "useless" things may lead to a long-term job. I mention this because there is a tendency for parents to ask me how to make their children interested in things that they can actually use later in life. Unfortunately, as I mentioned before, there is no way to force an interest, but there are many ways to steer in a direction that is employable, though you may have to think somewhat out of the box.

In my country, one autistic man has become a famous example among autism professionals. He had a special interest in knowing facts about popular music. If he were told to find a song, he knew the artist, album, year, and so on. For the longest time, he was employed at the national radio library, and his job was to find the albums they needed and put them back.

An interest in WWII weaponry could lead to employment in a museum, and an interest in grammar could lead to income in editing books, letters and much else in any number of firms of different kinds.

Toys, Games and Play

See also:
◇ School Parties and Birthdays ◇
◇ Special Interests ◇
◇ Self-Identity ◇

Kids love their toys and play games that are fun to them. There is nothing unusual about exploring the world through play. What may be very unusual about autistic children is the things about the world they feel the need to explore, and how many times they explore the same thing.

But like any other child, we play to have fun and to learn. We play to understand the world and explore narratives. Some of the things explored by other children through social contact, we may very well explore on our own instead. Do not worry about this. This is a part of our natural development.

ATTACHMENT TO TOYS

Autistic people usually have a great emotional attachment to certain objects. They also have a strong sense of justice, of right and wrong. Sometimes our logic can be hard to follow for other people, but it makes sense to us.

The objects we are attached to depend on age, special interest, and so forth. Almost every child has a favorite toy which is the best thing to play with and which they perhaps feel slightly territorial about. An autistic child also has favorite toys, but as with their room, their sense of what belongs to them is slightly more defined than you might expect. So, their reaction to another child playing with and perhaps breaking their toy will be greater and will last longer than that of their allistic peers.

> "I remember a birthday in my early childhood, I must have been six, maybe seven. It stands out in my mind as one of the first times I (or perhaps my parents) invited the children from my class to our house. Overall, the party went well until I discovered that the other children had been playing with my LEGO®, which in itself wasn't bad; what upset me was that they had taken apart my meticulously assembled constructions. This was a breach of trust which I could not bear, and as a result this was the only birthday I celebrated with non-family members until well into my teens, although by that time, this event was no longer my reason for not having a party, rather it had just never become a tradition for me to celebrate birthdays or other occasions with other students from my class." (Michael, personal communication)

An allistic child might get angry or sad in that same situation, but, in time, they will most likely want to have another party. An autistic child is set in their decision not only because they can be stubborn, but also because the betrayal or hurt experienced when other children have broken a toy of theirs is so great that it is not forgotten or forgiven easily. In other words, my favorite toy is more important to me than any number of birthday parties. In this regard, it also matters that to us, a birthday party is not necessarily fun, especially if it includes, as it does in some cultures, forced socialization and play with classmates rather than only the children we consider to be friends.

THE GAMES WE PLAY

Our choice of games and play is different than that of our allistic peers, and our reaction to being made to play under the rules of others is also different. We may play with toys expected of our gender, but often not in the same manner. Girls, if they are interested in dolls at all, will often use them to recreate a social interaction from their day repeatedly, in an attempt to understand what happened, rather than making up their own stories. Boys may play with LEGO® but be much more focused on the details of what they are building and will more often leave their creations standing. Building or setting something up can be the whole game for us, rather than "actually playing" with the toys, as Liane Holliday Willey discusses in her book, *Pretending to be Normal*:

> Like with my tea parties, the fun came from setting up and arranging things. Maybe this desire to organize things rather than play with things, is the reason I never had a great interest in my peers. They always wanted to use the things I had so carefully arranged. They would want to rearrange and redo. They did not let me control the environment. They did not act the way I thought they should act. Children needed more freedom than I could provide them. (Willey 1999, pp.16–17)

Autistic children seem perhaps to be less concerned with the gender expectations associated with specific toys, and more occupied with how much fun they are to us, or what we might learn by playing with them.

Most importantly, the games tend not to involve others. If games are social in nature, such as roleplaying games, or pretend games with other children involved, we may want or try to control what they do, so we don't get surprised. Letting another person control a character is a wildcard, as they may have other plans for the game which will then leave us confused and trying to catch up with the thought process of another, rather than enjoying the game.

I recall attempting to let a friend into one of my games and finding it, at times, perfectly fine. However, I also recall much greater joy playing the same game on my own, because there was less energy spent on trying to anticipate what my friend would do, and more on simply enjoying the game. Social games will often be either exact or very close re-enactments of observed events or something on television: either a story we love or a part of a story that contains something we do not quite understand. Re-enacting it gives us the chance to either re-experience the joy of the story at will, or attempt to learn, through repetition, whatever it is we do not understand.

We may also invent our own worlds, taking inspiration from other stories or building something from scratch. These worlds can be highly complicated and detailed, and we have no trouble remembering facts and details from this created world. I have heard concerns from parents that this world either takes over the child's whole life, social and otherwise, or that perhaps the child is not able to differentiate between make-believe and reality. In both cases, I would generally not worry. The reason it seems to take over our lives is because it becomes a special interest like any other. The joy we experience there is so great that nothing can match it. A reason it may seem that an autistic person cannot tell a made-up world from reality, can be that we enjoy the other world so much that we may at times "check out" of reality and refuse to participate. This is likely to pass on its own, and otherwise we can, for the most part, be baited back into reality by someone asking us about the world we have created. Social interaction can be easily initiated in this way, and from there, it can evolve. Whether done by an adult or a child does not matter in this case. What does matter is that we are not ridiculed for the created world, but instead complimented on our creativity. Another way is if we feel understood in our enthusiasm for it, or in our difficulties in the real world. Usually, if we do "check out" from reality, a part of that has to do with how stressful reality is. Keep in mind that the world your child has created, may lead them to create the next Harry Potter or Lord of the Rings.

Some children engage in writing their own fiction from a relatively early age, and again, this can be extensive and detailed and if a special interest includes, for example, the creation of a world or fascination with a character, we may be deeply intrigued with writing genealogies, descriptions and lists and drawing maps.

Again, these are solitary activities, but should not be discouraged for that reason. These are activities that bring us joy and help us to develop and increase skills that may be very useful in life.

In the playground, we tend to be on the periphery, observing rather than joining in. We may also actively hide from the other children, finding a quiet area. This may be due to bullying but can just as easily be a matter of the playground being a stressful sensory environment for us.

Even board games are turned into solitary games, by playing all sides ourselves. In Monopoly, we may choose to play as two or more players, actively trying to defeat each player's opponents. We do this to develop game strategies, but also to have a chance to experience the game without the social aspect and potential ridicule, should we lose. By playing all sides ourselves we always win, and therefore do not have to feel defeated, which, of course, is more common amongst children who have been bullied or ridiculed in this context, but worth mentioning to avoid the confusion that a child displaying this behavior "wants someone to play with" or is "lonely." They are experiencing the game in a way that feels safe to them. Alone does not equate to being lonely.

COMPUTER GAMES

With the increase in the amount of computer games available, and the young age at which many children begin playing, I feel it is important to include a section on this, specifically.

Many games are solitary and do not include social activity of any kind; however, this does not mean that your child cannot learn skills from playing. Many games require logic, the ability to think quickly, to recognize patterns, and so on: all skills that many autistic children are naturally good at. Such games should be encouraged, though possibly in some moderation, depending on the child's age.

It is also, in many cases, beneficial for an adult to engage in the game with the child, to help them understand the rules of the game, and keep their confidence up when training skills that the child is not good at. Compliment intelligence and creativity and encourage a positive view of mistakes.

When the child reaches an age where games like online multiplayer games such as World of Warcraft (WoW) or Conan can be played, I feel these and others like them should be encouraged for one reason in particular: This is the sort of game we can play while learning social skills and using them in real time.

A teenage or adult mentor can have their own account and play with the child, using the private chat functions (in WoW, this is called a whisper) to explain social rules when needed, as well as any game mechanics the child does not yet know. This type of game excludes the need to read voice intonation, facial expression and body language, so social interaction requires much less energy and can therefore be participated in for greater lengths of time, and without the consequence of social exhaustion at least to the same degree. If the games include emotes, any animation is often exaggerated and easy to understand, and text-based emotes are often very simple or highly descriptive, both of which can be helpful for us.

The problem can be some measure of addiction to the game, in part because the people we meet online can be our only perceived friends for long periods of time, and in part because we can become very good at it and be praised by online friends and acquaintances, and therefore feel a sense of achievement and social acceptance which is rare in the "real world."

As a parent, you must understand that the friends made online are real people, and if we have an appointment with them in the game, to meet for roleplaying or raiding or whatever it might be, the responsibility we feel to uphold the agreement is just as real as we would feel towards any other person. Obviously, feeling such responsibility is a good personality trait, and should therefore be encouraged, as it naturally would be if the appointment was to go to someone's house for a playdate. It should also be encouraged that the child informs you of their appointments with online friends, especially if they influence, for example, when your child may need to leave the dinner table. What should not be encouraged is neglecting "real world" friends in favor of online ones. Keep in mind that "real world" friends can also be engaged with through this medium, and that it may be a good way to socialize, due in part to the text-based conversation. Jimmi, a man with Asperger's, gave me his opinion on this topic, saying:

> "Some of the positives about playing computer games is that you can unwind and use it as downtime, that you can

> strengthen your ability to focus and get better at English [if you are not a native speaker]. For people with ASD it's also an easy way to be social, because you are doing something specific together. It can also be a good escape from reality, if you are pressured in real life." (Jimmi, personal communication)

Depending on the child's age, keep in mind whether previous special interests have become more moderate in time, and regulate your own response to the amount of time played accordingly. It works best to show interest and find ways to turn the interest into something that takes place in the "real world." For example, when your child is old enough, you may suggest going with them to a gaming convention where they can meet people who also love these games.

Computer games do not have to be social, however. A young autistic woman explained that she uses certain games to de-stress:

> "The right computer game is a blessing. It gives a feeling of repetition, a puzzle which on a very stressful day can untangle the mental ball of yarn. World of Warcraft, Ookami and Assassins Creed are really good for this purpose, I think. Other computer games drain me of energy, and I can only play them on good days. These are more complicated games with a high pace, which I have to think about or that have storylines." (Signe, personal communication)

HOW YOU CAN HELP

Accept that your child is not going to play the way other children do. Engage in conversation about the games and toys that have their interest. Do not force your involvement in the game, but make yourself available. By showing interest in your child's interest you teach them to interact with others about it, and they may be more inclined to make their interest a part of their social life. You also show them that you are interested in what they are doing, which likely makes them very happy. It is vital that you show and say that your child's choice of toys, manner of play and whatever level of engagement with other children, is good, intelligent and creative, because of possible criticism your child may meet from other adults.

You, as a parent, cannot do much to counter any bullying, but you can counter the comments made by teachers and other professionals, as well as those made by family members, who may feel the need to correct your child and their play.

Your child must know that you are supportive of whether they want to play with certain children, that you trust their judgment in choice of play-partners, that you like their choice of toy and think their way of playing is no less valuable than that of other children. They must know this, so that when a teacher tells them how to play and who to play with, they know that they always have you on their side, while, of course, they still have to be polite and respectful to both the teacher and other children.

Animals

See also:
◇ Theory of Mind and Social Reasoning ◇
◇ Chores ◇

Most autistic people respond very well to having animals around them, and many even express liking animals better than people. This is probably because animals seem much less complicated and unpredictable in their behavior than people do. They can become a lifelong special interest and a career, and they can be instrumental at reducing stress and anxiety.

In countries where therapy animals can be given to autistic children, many gain enormous benefit from having a therapy dog or cat. These benefits can be social, too, as a dog or cat may take direct attention, giving the autistic person some "space," or an animal can serve as a pathway to brief, positive social interactions with others. It is important to note that other animals, not just dogs and cats, can be therapeutically beneficial for an autistic person too.

LEARNING EMPATHY AND THEORY OF MIND

Animals in general, but especially mammals, are a great introduction to learning and practicing skills in empathy and Theory of Mind, namely, understanding the emotions of others and pinpointing where the emotion originates from, as well as figuring out what might fix a negative emotion for the pet.

With an animal such as a cat or dog, it is rather easy to tell if they are happy, excited, angry, scared, tired, surprised, and so on. Such animals provide an easy introduction to emotions and their origins. The dog is happy because you came home from school; it missed you. The dog is anxious because you are taking its bone away, and it really likes the bone and wants it back. When you are sad, very often a cat or dog will attempt to comfort you (other mammals will do this, too) even though it does not know why you are sad. This provides an avenue for you to talk with your child about how the animal knew they were sad, and how it tried to comfort them, even though it did not know or understand why they were sad.

There is also an easy introduction to Theory of Mind, in that the dog has to learn tricks; it does not magically know what you want it to do. Its behavior is relatively easy to predict and the spectrum of emotional reactions is perhaps less nuanced (as far as we know), and therefore easier to deal with as a concept.

CARETAKING

Another concept that is learnt in practical ways is caretaking. This is most especially true if your child is around very young animals, or even assists in caring for them. I personally grew up with a dog kennel. We had new puppies to take care of once or twice a year, and since I can remember, I have been involved in taking care of puppies from they were born until they were around eight weeks old, as well as the adult dogs.

This taught me about caretaking in a very concrete manner. For example, the puppies had to be weighed every day. Why? To make sure they were gaining weight. Why? Because this would mean they were eating and growing as they should.

I helped to clean up their business, because this has to be done to make sure their living environment is healthy. And the list goes on. There were good and logical reasons for doing everything that needed doing for both puppies and adult dogs. I helped cut their nails, brush them, teach them cleanliness, socialize with them and exercise them, mostly running around the lawn in my case, due to my aversion to being in public.

This all taught me about basic needs and fulfilling them, not to satisfy myself, but to take care of another living being.

In learning this, you also learn to postpone your own needs in favor of the pet's. It cannot wait an hour to take a walk because it has to go now. It needs your attention, your care, your time, which means you have to learn how to fulfil that need while temporarily ignoring your own. Your child will need your guidance to learn this, just as an allistic child will.

I am sure that learning these skills could also be achieved through helping with a baby, provided your child is old enough when the baby arrives. In learning these skills, what matters are the logical reasons to do things, combined with the next point.

BUILDING CONNECTIONS

You build a connection with this living being that is in your care. You learn slowly, over time, what makes them happy, excited and playful, and what makes them relax. They reciprocate in ways that are easy to understand, given a little education about the animal. A cat bumping you with its head, or a dog bringing you a toy when you are sad, sleeping in bed with you or curling up at your feet; either protecting you or being protected, feeling safe. Slowly, a relationship builds and what is very much a friendship emerges.

For a child who is stressed out from trying to deal with people, their emotions and language, their unfathomable reasons for doing things, and their frustrating, constant urge to speak, it is a considerable relief to be able to snuggle up on the couch and have your animal join you silently, asking for nothing from you. Likewise, it is a relief to have that animal come and want to play, because at least you know how to play this game, and you know how to tell if the animal is happy with you or not.

This is a safe friend: one that will never betray you, one that is always happy to see you. It is one that seems to understand you when no one else does, because they do not question your emotions or ask anything of you when you have nothing left to give. They support you just as you support them. In this way, the reciprocity of a friendship with an animal is very simple and easy to grasp for an autistic child.

All in all, though sometimes it is a chore to walk your dog at

5am in the rain or snow, the benefits of having an animal around are incredible and invaluable.

For many autistic people, animals are great company, very often preferred to that of humans because it is company we can bear.

> "To be honest, I probably like animals more than humans. I'm a vegetarian, an animal rights activist (when I have energy for it) and I want to be a vet after school. I've loved animals for as long as I can remember and they never cease, no matter if it's a spider or puppy, to put a smile on my face. I think it's because animals are a lot easier to understand than humans. People are so difficult to read and comprehend, while animals are honest and they do not judge you like people do. That's my kind of company." (Ellen, personal communication)

◇ Section 5 ◇

Identity

Self-Identity

See also:
◇ Co-Morbidity ◇
◇ Neurodiversity ◇
◇ Profiles ◇

WHO AM I?

When your behavior mimics that of others to the extent that it does for some autistic children, it can become quite difficult to discern who you are from the person or persons you mimic. This can be especially true for girls, as they are more prone to using that form of social adaptation. We can begin to question if we like the things we do because they like them, or because we like them. Do I wear the same clothes because it is pretty or because I am trying to be normal? This usually does not last for many years, but it ends up taking a lot of time and energy to deal with, nonetheless.

What you can do as a parent is to point out aspects of their personality and preferences from an early age and discuss how these are good things. The idea is not to force a certain identity on your child, or to force them away from the identity of the children and adults they mimic, but rather to instil confidence in your child that who they are, even if they adapt to social situations differently depending on where they are, is someone who is loved, appreciated and who has good values and characteristics.

With confidence should eventually come the ability to shed some of the mask and march to their own beat.

FEELING ALIEN AND INTEREST COMMUNITIES

One factor which can affect identity is autism, and the diagnosis of ASD. Because of the experiences with social difficulties, sensory processing differences, their interests not being understood or appreciated by others, or repetitive behaviors not being accepted, autistic people can feel that they are wrong or "other." This is, for some, a very difficult feeling to cope with, as there can be a sense that there is no hope of creating connections with others. It can also become a part of someone's identity to be entirely other, not belonging to "mainstream society," or to belong to a small community of people who identify as outsiders in some way. Sometimes, these communities identify themselves by their being excluded from mainstream society and attempts at reaching out and showing acceptance can be met with suspicion. However, for the most part, such communities are defined by their interests in something specific which is, more or less, not mainstream. It could also be interests which are becoming more widely accepted, such as gaming, anime, or being fans of particular shows, music or books.

Becoming engaged in such communities is often a way to find not only social interaction and friendship, but also a sense of belonging and being accepted somewhere. This means that, unless the interest is harmful or hateful in some way, it is likely bringing a great deal of good to your child's life and should not be discouraged. Even if you might perceive it as odd, this is an example of your child discovering and exploring their identity. In fact, seeking out communities to belong to is one of the most normal ways of doing this. The only real difference will be the focus interest or activity of the community which, in your child's case, is more likely to be outside of the mainstream and often connected closely to their special interest.

DIAGNOSIS

Being diagnosed with ASD can set in motion thoughts of being wrong as well. In the diagnostic language and its connotations, the focus is on what a person cannot do, has difficulties with, or in which ways they are "other than." For this reason, being diagnosed can enhance feelings of otherness, or can set in motion an identity crisis. Is this who I am, now and forever? Does ASD/autism define me?

It is important to help your child understand that a diagnosis does not change who they are; it merely helps increase understanding of particular difficulties which already existed, and helps those around you understand some of the behaviors which people might not have understood. A diagnosis is a tool to understand and communicate to the people around them the ways in which they may need accommodations. It can lessen confusion and give access to help in their daily life.

However, it is not the entirety of who they are. It is a piece of it.

Many autistic people prefer to say that they are autistic rather than having autism, precisely because they do perceive autism as being intrinsic to their identity. However, this does not mean that they—or I—mean that autism is all that we are. Instead, what it means is that it is an essential part of who we are, which cannot be taken away from us and which shapes our way of being in the world and experiencing it.

But identity is much more than that.

IDENTITIES ARE COMPLEX

Identity is a whole picture with lots of pieces. As an autistic person, sometimes our literal way of thinking can make it tricky to put our identity into words. We can get caught up in thinking of ourselves in a way that centers on specific topics. This can be linked to a special interest or our diagnosis, or it could be centered on the role of being a student, or daughter/son, and so on.

However, a person's identity is comprised of so many pieces. In fact, the puzzle piece analogy may be very useful here. An identity puzzle might have 100 pieces—just as an example. Each piece has a name: nationality, roles in life, interests, personality characteristics, neurology (such as being autistic), social characteristics, or whatever else you can think of.

When talking about identity, it is important to emphasize that each piece is just one part of who that person is as a whole. Each piece matters. Not necessarily equally, but each carries importance in the bigger picture of the puzzle.

Remember also that identity is fluid and dynamic. For some people, there are periods in their lives when their identity changes a lot in the span of five years. Many adults will remember having a different sense of identity in their teens, or being confused about their identity. For autistic people, there can sometimes be no question at all, or it can be a very chaotic process to figure out what that puzzle looks like.

Aging, Growing Up and Puberty

See also:
◇ Friends ◇
◇ Bullying and Peer Pressure ◇
◇ Social Media ◇
◇ Self-Identity ◇

Puberty and the years surrounding it are confusing and difficult for everyone. Hormones, physical development and social changes are some of the major themes, no matter if you are autistic or not. But for autistic people, these things can be difficult in different ways, or the difficulties can be more extreme.

HORMONES AND PHYSICAL CHANGES

When talking about puberty, a lot of people will first think of "hormones." However, they think of it in a colloquial sense wherein the word is used more to refer to the emotional chaos surrounding physical, sexual and social changes that occur around that time. Of course, hormones are connected to all of this, and this is all well and normal.

One part of what happens is growing and the body shape changing: new hair growth, acne, and so on. It is all "part of the package" of puberty. For autistic people, the sometimes-rapid changes, and the fact that changes are happening, can be deeply distressing. First of all, growing pains can be very real. It can hurt or feel uncomfortable to be in your own body in an entirely new way. You have no idea when it will stop, either, which makes it all the more distressing. Second, your body changing to look different can be distressing in several ways. One is that change is happening at all. You are used to your body looking one way and that image is linked to the recognition of yourself in the mirror. Suddenly changes are happening very quickly and you do not look like yourself or feel like yourself. Distress about these changes is not necessarily a sign of gender dysphoria, but it can be. However, often it is a reaction to change and unpredictability. Changes are happening which you have no control over at all.

For those who develop menstrual periods, there are many aspects which can add to confusion and distress. Menstrual cramps can be brutal, as most people who have had them can attest to. For many, the first few years with cramps are the worst, though hormonal birth control can lessen the symptoms significantly. However, living through cramps which feel like your insides are breaking apart is very distressing indeed. Knowing that your growing breasts are related to that can make the breasts a part of the problem in your mind, and lead to not wanting them at all. Aside from cramps, there is the aspect that you are actually bleeding, and tactile sensitivities can be triggered by those sensations, and by wearing pads or tampons. Additionally, new social standards are suddenly applied to you, including different expectations of how you should act and dress. Things that were perfectly normal and okay before suddenly are not. An example is the expectation that you will now wear bras, which are a very uncomfortable garment (I believe anyone with breasts who has worn bras will agree at least to some extent). This then carries its own set of sensory sensitivities and social confusion with it. Why do I need to wear this? It is not nice to wear, it feels different on my skin. Perhaps it even feels painful. Generally, wearing sports bras can be a way to meet these expectations halfway, but this may still be highly uncomfortable for those who do not like to wear tight-fitting clothing items.

For those with penises, there will be new sensations and reactions—sometimes involuntary—to deal with, and this can cause great distress too. This is especially true for involuntary erections which may occur in front of other people, as these situations can lead to feeling embarrassed, or even to being teased or bullied.

Sexual maturity and curiosity may develop in a way that is not outwardly expressed through clothing or behavior, but remains—for longer than typical—more of an inner world. Where allistic peers may sooner change their clothing choices and behaviors to match their new emotions, autistic people may not make these same changes, or not to the same degree. They are less likely to have their inner world reflected by their behavior or appearance in the same way, or this change may take much longer. There is nothing wrong with this of course, but as a parent you should be aware that these changes may be happening in your child without them talking about it or reflecting it in another way. Your child may need to express or talk about these changes for a long time before they feel comfortable with embracing new parts of their own identity.

SOCIAL CHANGES AND EMOTIONS

There may also be a great deal of confusion about the changes in their friends or classmates as their behaviors and interests change, and your child can feel suddenly disconnected from people who used to be close friends.

Children who, just a year ago, were still playing with toys or watching children's movies suddenly become interested in new types of movies, books and celebrities, or start to express their gender in new ways, and this affects friendships. If an autistic child has the same special interest but their peers have moved on, those friendships feel lost. There can even be a sense of betrayal.

Autistic people can mature at a different rate than their allistic peer group or, as mentioned, the changes to their inner world may not be reflected outwardly. This can be unsettling and confusing. I recall around age 12 or 13 how girls in my class wore make-up and spoke about boys, and I wanted friends but my interest in, for example, boybands, was (still) rooted in their music. This meant that I could not really participate well in the conversations, even if the overall topic was the same as my interest. This can happen even if sexual curiosity has begun to develop, as that curiosity may not be connected in our minds to interests where it would have been for allistic peers, such as an interest in a particular celebrity.

There can, of course, be a beginning interest in love, romantic relationships and sex, but it may be difficult to know how to express it. This is true for many allistic people, too, but with the added social difficulties or differences in autistic people, it can become so frightening to even try to express emotions or curiosity that we may stop ourselves from doing so. A large part of the emotional difficulties in puberty are often related to poor interoception; we can have such a difficult time recognizing that we are feeling something and what that feeling is, that we either do not realize that anything is happening, or we wrongly (or over-) interpret our own thoughts and feelings. Recognizing, for example, the difference between being physically or romantically attracted to someone and simply being very fond of their company can be tricky. Some people may even become special interests for us, which can be very confusing and difficult, as such an "obsessive" feeling can be difficult to distinguish from a crush or "being in love," especially as portrayed in media.

> "I used to think I got a lot of crushes on people, like a new one every day. But as an adult, I've realized that these were actually 'friendship-crushes.' I wasn't actually in love, but thought they were really awesome, and I wanted to be close to them and talk to them. It was so confusing as a teenager to believe that I was in love with all these people and probably pushed a lot of people away by being too intense. Now, as an adult, I can see that I just did not understand my own feelings at the time." (Andie, personal communication)

> "Making the distinction between physical and romantic attraction was especially difficult during adolescence. I could easily recognize when others felt attraction towards me, because it was overwhelming to say the least, but being overwhelmed only compounded the general confusion I felt in terms of how to react appropriately. Often, I found it hard to even make facial expressions, much less speak, as my muscles felt as though they had been exposed to cold temperatures, very numb and stiff." (Scott, personal communication)

Gender and Sexual Identity

See also:
◇ **Friends** ◇
◇ **Self-Identity** ◇
◇ **Aging, Growing Up and Puberty** ◇

Sometimes, people can be uncomfortable talking about these topics, and especially when there is disability or neurodiversity involved. I have actually had people question whether I can have a sex life at all, being autistic. But autistic people are sexual beings, too, just like non-autistic people are. We also have gender identity, and we are capable of expressing it and advocating for ourselves.

There is a larger proportion of the autistic population, relative to the general population, who are not cisgender (someone whose gender corresponds to the sex assigned at birth) and/or heterosexual. That is, a larger percentage of us feel and identify as a different gender than the body we were born with, and a larger percentage are not attracted to the opposite gender, or at least not only to the opposite gender

SEXUAL DEVELOPMENT AND VULNERABILITY

Children and adolescents with ASD develop hormonally at the same pace as neurotypicals, but there may be a delayed emotional maturity. This can cause some issues, in terms of identity and vulnerability.

Usually, confusion and misunderstandings can arise when the children and adolescents around them begin developing their sexual identities and their behavior begins to change. Different clothes are expected if you want to be cool, and peer pressure can take on new forms. Suddenly, everyone else is saying that they have already had their first kiss; others will claim to have done more, and because of your child's naivety, they will believe these things as true without question and think that this behavior is expected of them, much earlier than other children in some cases. This leads directly into the main point, which is vulnerability. As with bullying, we have no radar to spot predators. We also may not realize that it is okay to say no.

Some of us can very easily be overwhelmed by positive attention once someone gives it to us, and to the extent that we will do almost anything to maintain it. We are easily manipulated, especially because we will not always say no even when we want to scream and run. Thus, we are more likely to end up in situations where we cannot escape, and therefore, as a demographic, we are vulnerable to being sexually assaulted or even raped.

I do not mention this to scare you. You should not lock your child or adolescent up for the rest of their lives. Teach us that it is okay to say no, and teach us that this is the strong and smart thing to do in situations where we want to say no. Teach your child about how to stay safe, such as not to go off with a stranger, but instead to call someone they know and be picked up, or to call a taxi and tell them you will pay because otherwise, they might think they cannot afford this way to escape an uncomfortable situation. Teach them to give the wrong phone number if they need to get rid of someone—yes, teach them to lie! Things that may seem obvious to you will not occur to your child.

GENDER IDENTITY AND SEXUAL ORIENTATION

Another (rarer) problem in this category, is that if your child has a tendency to mimic others, they may choose social groups and even sexual orientations to mimic, taking it on as a part of their identity. This is usually a "Hey, those people are also not accepted by the mainstream so I'll just be one of them!"-reaction. This goes back to the earlier point about giving them confidence in who they are.

There may also be feelings of identifying with the "otherness" that the social group experiences. Connecting with that otherness in other people can be an intense experience at first and may lead to over-identifying with that group for some time. A strong sense of identity can help your child to figure out in which ways they do or do not identify with the social group.

Also, like allistic adolescents, figuring out who you are is a learning curve, so they may figure out later that this is not them. There can also be an obsession with or special interest in a sexual orientation or gender identity. It can come across as very simplified or caricatured. "I like dolls and dresses, so I must be a girl" or "I like having my hair short and I like playing sports so I must be a boy." In cases like this, it is important that the child learns about the differences between biological sex, gender identity, gender expression and sexual orientation. There are many places on the internet that provide information on this, for example, The Genderbread Person at www.ItsPronouncedMetrosexual.com gives a brief intro to the differences between and the spectrums of gender identity, gender expression, biological (or anatomical) sex and sexual orientation. (Note here that biological sex is not binary, as many have been taught in school. In fact, even chromosomal sex has many variants, not to mention hormones and physical attributes.)

Learning about this can help your child to think in a more nuanced way about their own identity. Because naturally, if your understanding of sex and gender boils down to girls = long hair and dresses, and boys = short hair and football, and you are a girl who likes your hair short, you may feel very confused. However, knowing about the spectrum of gender expression can alleviate that confusion.

However – and this is a big however:

For the most part, if your child tells you they are gay, bisexual, asexual or any other sexuality, it is probably because they have done their research and truly feel this way. Likewise, if they tell you that they are genderfluid or that they are a different gender from their assigned one, they have likely thought about it for a long time and done extensive research. Finding words that describe our identity can be very important, especially because of the feelings of otherness that we often experience.

Furthermore, if young children express clear signs of gender dysphoria, such as wanting to remove their penis, this is a pointer that it should be taken seriously.

For autistic people, the feelings of otherness can make it easier to recognize other ways in which you are different, such as being transgender, because breaking with the "norm" is already an experience you know well. For this reason, many autistic children and adolescents already may feel very comfortable and confident in their non-cis gender identity. However, being autistic can also make it very difficult to realize that struggling to fit in with an imposed gender identity is the reason for your feeling not quite right about yourself. Some will live very long lives before they find that "missing piece."

> "For many years I lived with the notion I must be 'middle sex'... I didn't feel female, I didn't look male, so I must be somewhere in between. I knew I felt very male, but my body seemed to say otherwise. Many years later I came to understand gender is based within the neurological system, it's a 'brain thing.' So, my body might look female but my gender identity is male. It was like a light went on and the reality gushed into me like a river racing toward the ocean. Once I had acted upon that recognition and moved my body to fit my gender (medical transition that took a few years) I experienced for the first time what being 'home' felt like! In today's current technological age, I can't change my brain to fit my body, but I can change my body to fit my brain." (Dr. Wenn B. Lawson (PhD) PCychol AFBPsS MAPS, personal communication)

The proportion of autistic people who identify as asexual is also much higher than in the general population. Being asexual is very different from being celibate. If you are celibate, you have sexual attractions but do not act on them, whereas someone who is an asexual has no desire to be sexually active with anyone, though many still want life partners. This is, again, a spectrum and not nearly as simple as I've described it here, but this is the quick gist of it.

I include this to let you know that any of these thoughts and ideas should be taken seriously. Once your child comes and tells you, you can generally assume that they probably know what they are talking about, and have thought about it a great deal, and therefore you should do your best to react in a neutral or positive manner. Reacting in a negative way can have serious, long-term consequences for your relationship, and for the self-esteem and self-worth of your child.

It is important to know that the suicide (attempt) rate is very high in people with gender dysphoria, which means that your acceptance and support are paramount.

Helping your child to find their own identity is mostly about speaking openly about these things and allowing them to hear people talk about their experiences. Recognize also that stereotypes can be very harmful and not conducive to a healthy development of identity. As with neurodiversity, we are coming to understand that no two gender and sexual identities are the same, as we all lie somewhere on the spectrums of biological/anatomical sex, gender identity, gender expression and sexual attraction/orientation. Whoever you are, and whoever your child is, everyone is diverse and unique and everything is normal and human.

LEARNING ABOUT SEXUALITY AND SEXUAL BEHAVIOR

Sexual development and social awkwardness are never the greatest combination, but that doesn't mean that autistic people cannot have good and healthy knowledge about sexuality, sexual behavior and relationships. Many children are not given appropriate sex education, including autistic children, and this section cannot cover everything. But below are a few relevant points to consider.

Teaching appropriateness is a good place to start. Social rules regarding sexual behavior, which may be obvious (but not spoken about) to others, may not be obvious to an autistic person. Try to be precise, but if your child can learn to generalize knowledge, it will be good to have conversations which encourage the generalization of appropriate behavior.

Autistic people can be impulsive in their behavior, and can have poor interoception, also in relation to their own sexual desire. This can result in unfortunate circumstances. It can also mean that some of the sexual behavior they may see in movies, such as the hero suddenly kissing the woman without asking consent, may need to be subject to conversations about appropriateness and impulsive behavior, and about consent and communication.

Teaching consent and communication is very important—not just for autistic people, but also for allistic people. There are many online sources which can help with this, and if your child is good at understanding metaphors, there are child-appropriate comics and videos which employ metaphors. One is the "Tea and Consent" video, which takes under three minutes. This one may be more appropriate for adolescents and younger adults, but you can search for it and check it out yourself first to see whether you want to show it to your child and discuss it with them. There are also videos about consent made specifically for autistic people, which are available for free on sites like YouTube.

Do not punish behavior that is human and not harmful. That is, if your child is not harming someone, then it is okay. It is normal to explore your own sexuality, your own identity, your own expression. This is human behavior, and unless what they are doing is illegal—such as exposing themselves in public—or harmful—such as touching others without consent—then it will be better to remain open and supportive. Of course, the examples given are situations that would be very clear, so consider the situations which are relevant to you and your child and keep communicating!

Importantly, when it comes to consent, your child's consent must also be respected. One way in which children are taught to cross their own boundaries are when adults react negatively to the child not wanting to hug or kiss family members. The child learns that others will force them to do physically intimate things which they do not want to do, and that this is socially acceptable. In this way, a child can learn not to listen to their own feelings about what they do or do not want to consent to.

Please remember that your child's learning about consent starts long before you talk about sex or sexual behavior and teach them that their boundaries matter.

One last point which I want to include is regarding emotions. It can be very difficult to understand that if you feel something, others might not. Likewise, others may feel something that you do not. Learning about this, and what to do with conflicts that may arise, is something your child may need guidance in. There is also a point about emotion permanence. In the same vein as object permanence, some autistic people experience that if a person is not around, physically, the emotions attached to that person can move into the background, even if that person is still deeply loved and a primary person in their lives. An example of this:

> "My husband is currently studying abroad. We've been together for many years and will definitely live together again, but circumstances right now mean that we live apart. It has renewed an interesting feature of how my emotions work that I hadn't expected... Whenever we haven't seen each other for a few weeks, it's like I have to get to know him again and get to know our emotional bond again. It doesn't take very long, but it happens every time. It doesn't mean I love him any less, but it's like my emotions need a reminder anyway. It's like this with friendships, too." (Anonymous, personal communication)

In some cases, as explained here, the emotions connected to that person are re-awakened in a short period of time once the person is there again. In others, the connection may feel instant. With regard to friendships, many autistic people have friendships in which there is no communication at all for months or even years, but the emotions connected to that person have not dampened; instead they have been "parked" while the person was not available or communication was not active. This happens in romantic relationships as well, which can be difficult for a romantic partner to understand. Again, communication is most often the key.

Meltdowns and Shutdowns

See also:
◇ **Amygdala and Emotions** ◇
◇ **How to Give Advice** ◇
◇ **What Helps in the Big Picture?** ◇

Meltdowns and shutdowns are both common in autistic people, and while each person usually will tend toward one or the other, everyone can experience either. This is important because others (and even we ourselves) can label us as inward or outward reactive with the implication that this means that we only have meltdowns or shutdowns. In reality, people do not work like that. Personally, during my whole life, I can remember only two meltdowns and countless shutdowns, but even this very skewed statistic still leaves the possibility that I will someday react outwardly again.

It is difficult to fully describe what a meltdown or shutdown is, because they are different for each person. Descriptions here are, therefore, necessarily incomplete.

WHAT DOES IT LOOK AND FEEL LIKE?

Meltdowns can include getting very angry, uncontrolled crying, running away, becoming outwardly aggressive/physical, beginning to stim uncontrollably. Shutdowns can include crying or becoming completely passive in expression, either not moving at all or only moving to stim, often close to the body or with small movements, rocking back and forth, or cradling into the fetal position.

Both often include being unable to process information, which means that if someone is speaking to you, you are often unable to understand what is being said or it will take a lot longer than usual to understand and form any type of reply. Speech can be very difficult, and so any questions should be yes or no questions, and only asked if absolutely necessary. Both can happen seemingly very quickly and usually last around 15–30 minutes. Some are much shorter, and some much longer. Again, this is individual.

It is important to note that aggressive behavior during a meltdown is not intentional and it will not help to punish it afterwards. There is a big difference between intentional aggressive behavior and being so overloaded that you are no longer in control.

Meltdowns and shutdowns feel different for every person, and for that reason, they are difficult to sum up. Some describe them as an ongoing electric shock, or like imploding, disintegrating, dissociating from yourself, you feel like you are not "you" anymore, a storm of emotions, complete despair, or a hole of numbness. Some black out entirely, as their brain is overloaded to the point that memory encoding apparently stops functioning. For some, there can be early warning signs, such as "aura"-like impressions like those people get before a migraine; some will feel their body start to shiver or shake, feel a tingling or prickly sensation, become dizzy beforehand, or feel their breathing begin to change, often towards hyperventilation. Others may not feel any warning signs at all.

For those who feel meltdowns or shutdowns building, they can feel so inevitable and overpowering that there is no glimpse of hope. Scott wrote to me that:

> "In the worst cases, attempting to prevent a meltdown is like trying not to get wet from rising floodwater, equipped only with yet-to-be-filled sandbags, each one having more holes in it than the last. Also, you can't swim.
>
> Generally, meltdowns occur when overstimulated, behind schedule, and unable to communicate or locate something important. Shutdowns generally occur during moments of personal failure, though even the slightest mistakes can

> accumulate over time and cause one worse than mentioned above. I have had people enter my field of vision and wave, as if to say 'Are you there?' and I noticed but no response could reach the surface, not even in recognition." (Scott, personal communication)

It is important to note that having a meltdown or shutdown feels awful. I want to recognize that witnessing it is distressing as well, of course. However, sometimes we forget to talk about how horrible it is to experience, and how draining it is. It is often something that we feel for several days afterwards.

> "I am normally more inward-reactive, but I do have meltdowns sometimes. For example, in one instance I was very stressed already and then some plans were changed. I couldn't cope and ended up spiraling into a meltdown. When I have meltdowns, I feel a need to bite something and, in this instance, I ended up biting a bunch of magazines—I used to end up biting myself instead and hurting myself, so I'm thankful that with age I am able to channel it in a way that is not harmful to myself or others. But it is still very uncomfortable and I can feel the effects for up to several days later. Recovery takes a shorter time if I am allowed the solitude I need." (Andie, personal communication)

The after-effects of a meltdown or shutdown can last for a few minutes or several days, as Andie describes. It may be fatigue, emotional numbness or over-sensitivity, dizziness, intense headaches; sensory sensitivities are often heightened such that it feels like every sense is hyper-exposed. Often, we will be more prone to another meltdown or shutdown in the following days as we are close to overload, and still "healing" from the event.

While I understand that this can seem like a poor excuse, there is actually good reason for it. When the stress system is overloaded to the point of triggering such an extreme emotional response, the stress hormones take time to be "flushed out." Adrenaline takes about 15–20 minutes from when the stressful situation has ended, but cortisol takes much longer. Importantly, there are studies that suggest that autistic people's stress systems, at the neurological level, may not shut down when it is supposed to, which can explain why it takes so much longer for us to regain our resilience to things like sensory or social input after a meltdown or shutdown.

HOW CAN I HANDLE IT?

As mentioned, communication will be much more difficult than it usually is, so avoid trying to talk about why this is happening or asking for proper responses to anything. Your child may be able to process enough to respond with shaking their head yes or no, but this is not certain. If they can do that, questions should not go beyond things like "Would you like your weighted blanket?" or "Should I turn off the lights?". Any questions about how they are feeling or what is going on is too much. Save it for when they are calm!

If you know the environment is stressful for your child, try to be extra attentive as being overwhelmed can gradually (sometimes on a steep curve) affect the person's ability to communicate their state and their needs. There may be small signs that you can notice but which the person themselves does not or cannot.

Generally, during a meltdown or shutdown, avoid touching the person unless they are self-harming. If they are self-harming, you should only touch them to stop the self-harming behavior, and only as a last resort. Other ways to help calm the situation down include:

Take a step back

Take a step back or leave the room entirely, but if you are leaving, say that this is what you are doing and that you are available when they need you. Inform of what is happening, no more, no less. An example: "I am going to leave the room to give you space. If you need me, I am right outside the door/in the living room." When your child is calm, and only when they are calm, you can speak with them about how they prefer you to handle meltdowns, how you can best help them to calm down and to get through the experience.

Provide a weighted blanket

Weighted blankets are, for many, helpful in regaining a sense of your own body, or can feel like a "protective layer" against the world. When you are having a meltdown or shutdown, these functions can be helpful to soothing your emotional state and the feeling of (controlled and predictable) pressure on your skin or body can help to focus the mind or it can feel like the chaos of the meltdown or shutdown is confined to the space of the blanket and not overflowing into the world. This description may be a bit strange, but this is the best summation I can provide, taking into consideration the different ways people relay their experience to me.

Provide a quiet and/or dark space

Turn off some of the lights, close the curtains, do not speak more than necessary. This is related to many of the same issues as the weighted blanket. Controlling sensory input as much as possible is an important factor in bringing down the energy or controlling the chaos that is going on for the person who has a meltdown or shutdown. For this reason, any aspect of sensory input you can control—and preferably minimize—will likely help. There will be some who prefer loud music or noise, but for most, in my experience, quiet and dark are go-to solutions.

> "... It seems like my brain just stops functioning. I can still see, hear, feel etc.—I still get sensory input—but it feels like this input doesn't really register with me. I also get the impression that my system is trying to dampen all of the sensory input. When I get overwhelmed by my senses, it feels more like an attack that is not dampened at all. All of the sensory input just keeps coming at me, and it is like there is no filtering. In such a case, I need to find a quiet place—or, if this is not possible, it can help me to take cover under blankets and use my ear plugs as well as noise-cancelling headphones. I can

> only recover by cutting off as much of the sensory input as possible. After such an experience of overload I am usually very, very tired and need a lot of rest to feel like myself again." (Sif, personal communication)

CATCHING THE SIGNS AND PREVENTATIVE TIPS

As mentioned, there can be early warning signs of meltdowns and shutdowns, such as "aura"-like impressions similar to those before a migraine, sensations of shivering or shaking, dizziness, or changes in breathing, often approaching hyperventilation. Not everyone experiences these warning signs or is able to register them. Some people can learn later in life to spot them and some cannot.

If you can catch warning signs, things like a weighted blanket or other controlled sensory input can be helpful in preventing the meltdown. Stimming can also be helpful to prevent a meltdown/shutdown or bring down the energy.

Generally, anything which usually brings down the stress level for that person can be used to attempt to avoid a full meltdown or shutdown. It will not always work, however, whenever it does not work, do not take this as a failure or a sign that the technique has stopped working. It may still work next time, and no one can prevent every meltdown or shutdown in their lives. Every time you succeed is great, and that should be the focus.

Harmful Strategies and Risky Behavior

See also:
◇ Bullying and Peer Pressure ◇
◇ Social Media ◇
◇ Aging, Growing Up and Puberty ◇

Because there is such a high risk of autistic people developing anxiety and depression, we must acknowledge the risk of also developing harmful coping strategies or engaging in risky behavior. These include, but are not limited to, overusing alcohol, using drugs, engaging in self-harm, isolating oneself, and contemplating, planning, attempting or dying by suicide.

All of these can be viewed, by the individual, as just trying to cope with the world or their problems, and it can indeed be very tempting to seek out things that will numb the pain.

I wish to reiterate at the beginning of this chapter that I am not a doctor or a specialist in this topic. The knowledge I am passing on here is somewhat basic neurology or common health advice. For this reason, it is not an in-depth explanation, and much of it is simplified. Please do your own research if you want to know more and remember to be sceptical of your sources.

DRUGS AND ALCOHOL

What is the actual issue with drugs and alcohol? Well, naturally, one of the effects is that alcohol and some drugs will provide a sense of numbing or being distant from the emotions that hurt. This prevents the person from actually processing those emotions, coping with them and moving on from them in a healthy way. Another problem that arises is that with use of any substance—legal or not—the body and brain get used to the substance and the person will experience the need for a higher dosage in order to achieve the same effect. This can be highly dangerous as it will lead the person to drink more or take a higher dose of drugs, because they still want to have the effect, but they can overdose by accident.

Yet another issue which results from alcohol or drug use is that because the brain and body must spend their energy on dealing with being poisoned, it can slow or even halt the development of the brain. For example, the connections within our frontal lobes—where we make informed decisions and control our actions—and between the frontal lobes and the limbic system—where our emotions and fear reactions are registered and processed, and where we "keep an eye on" if our body is feeling okay—do not finish developing until our mid-twenties. This means that our ability to control emotional outbursts or inward reactions, our ability to prioritize and make well-considered decisions can be affected not only while we feel the effects of the alcohol or drug, but also much later. This is, of course, especially true when the person drinks or uses often or in large amounts.

None of this is meant to say that if you (or your child) ever have a drink your brain will forever be harmed and you will never become functional. Of course not. However, it is not a good way to cope with anxiety or depression.

SELF-HARM AND SUICIDE

Self-harm creates several of the same problems that drugs and alcohol do. It looks different, of course, because it takes the form of someone harming their body in a physical, and usually visible, way. As with drugs and alcohol, the feelings that self-harming releases can become addictive, causing behavior to escalate. This is because the brain is releasing neurotransmitters and hormones that are slightly soothing, which is exactly what the person needs at that moment. It is a survival mechanism, but one which, in self-harm, becomes a part of a downward spiral. Self-harm may seem like a solution in the moment, but does nothing to actually treat the cause.

Note that self-harming does not necessarily mean that a person wants to die. Very often, it is the only way they can think of to deal with the emotional pain they are feeling. Making it physical and concrete. However, it can be a warning sign of suicidal ideation, and should be taken every bit as seriously. Even if it is not a sign of suicidal ideation, self-harm tends to escalate and can cause permanent disfigurement as well as permanent injuries such as nerve and tissue damage.

If you suspect your child is having suicidal thoughts, or they are self-harming, seek professional help quickly. If your child is still a minor, request support from someone trained to deal with children. This is important because children do not express the same symptoms as adults do, and their level of cognitive development must be taken into account when speaking to them. Staff trained to interview and treat children know how to approach these challenges. Equally important, seek assessment and treatment from professionals trained in autism: autistic children and adults may need to be asked about their thoughts and feelings in a different way, and someone who is not aware of this can miss important signs.

It is important to remember than people who go through self-harm or suicidal thoughts can become happy again. Whatever is going on, it is not permanent, even if they believe it is.

ISOLATION

If it is difficult to cope with the world and daily life, it may seem like the best option is to withdraw from it and isolate oneself. Unfortunately, this usually does not solve the problem.

It is important to note that having limited social contact can be the right thing for an autistic person's mental health. By isolation I mean having less contact with other people than what is healthy for that person: having very few or no close relationships with family, people with the same interests or anyone else. Having a close relationship, for an autistic person, may mean only speaking over text or online voice chats, it may mean that conversations are short and far between. Because of this, what qualifies as isolating oneself is dependent on what the behavior used to be, and whether the previous behavior allowed for good quality of life for the autistic person.

A person who is isolating themselves may at first feel better, because the stress of social interaction is gone. However, some of the good neurotransmitters and hormones we get from social interaction will also be gone, and over time, this contributes to depression and anxiety because, normally, those neurotransmitters and hormones act as a kind of buffer against depression and anxiety. The result is then that the person actually ends up feeling worse.

We can compare this to someone who seeks darkness, closing their curtains because they seek the feeling of being in a safe "cave." This is not immediately harmful, but if you do not get exposed to sunlight, it will be harder for you to get vitamin D—which yes, can be substituted with a pill—and it will be harder to maintain any sort of circadian rhythm, which can result in poorer sleep, excessive sleep and overall fatigue. In the same way, not getting access to positive social experiences (and it is important that they are positive) means that you do not get those hormones in your brain which contribute to your well-being.

One middle-ground can be a pet. Interacting with a dog, for example, can still provide these good hormones. As additional benefits, having a dog means having to go outside and get exposed to sunlight, getting exercise, and possibly having more short, positive social interactions when someone asks to pet your dog or what its name is. These little social scripts can be easier to rehearse and cope with than other random social encounters.

What Helps in the Big Picture?

There are "big fixes" in life. I am not talking about "curing" all our difficulties, but rather, improving overall physical and mental health. These "fixes" aren't things you learn to use effectively on your own until adulthood, if at all, which is why I want to tell you, the parents. When speaking to autistic people about what helps them in the bigger picture, it is very often the same things you will hear. I hope that by sharing them some children will reap the benefits earlier in life, and that this can assist in laying the foundation for a happy and successful life.

SO, WHAT REALLY HELPS?

Regular sleep and daylight

Most of us have trouble with sleep. Generally, what I hear, as well as experience myself, is that our minds wake up at night. Unfortunately, society does not agree with that. However, because it is so easy for us to be awake at night, and we get our best work done after sundown, it is essential that we have regular sleeping patterns and that our sleep is as good as possible. Getting enough daylight is really good for the brain and helps the brain maintain a regular sleeping pattern. The rhythm of daylight tells the brain when it is time to wake up, and when it is time to sleep. Giving your brain these cues for a day-rhythm goes a long way!

There are a few tools available. If it is not enough to simply have a routine with set sleeping hours that do not change during the weekend, along with getting plenty of daylight, you can try one or several of these options:

Taking extra vitamin D

Many of us are vitamin D deficient, as so many of us prefer to stay indoors as much as humanly possible and do not get enough sunlight. Taking some extra vitamin D can therefore help tremendously. Be aware that some people may have to take this along with calcium – ask your doctor.

Weighted blankets/duvets

Autistic adults have told me how these help them to gather themselves mentally, and help increase awareness of their body, providing a sense of being grounded and safe. They are especially good for those who have problems with the proprioceptive sense. There are duvets and blankets available with different forms of weight in them. Some are noisier than others, and some are heavier than others. See if this can be a solution. Many autistic people speak very highly of these, although some note that they sometimes have to change the weight. I know that some people keep two of them with different weight and change between the two according to their need.

Melatonin

I would only recommend taking extra melatonin during periods of difficulty falling asleep. Melatonin is not a conventional sleeping pill, but is more of a sleep regulator, mostly used in circadian rhythm disorders. Circadian rhythm disorders are when a person is unable to sleep and wake at the normal times required for school, work and social needs. These types of disorders are common in autistic people, though it is not known exactly why. Melatonin is one of the treatments used for these types of disorders. Melatonin is only proven to have a moderate effect in patients above the age of 55. This could mean either that the effect described by so many autistic people is the result of a placebo effect, or that we perhaps react differently to it than the general population, and there simply are no studies to show this. I cannot tell you which it is, I can only tell you my experience and what I have heard from other autistic people. My experience is that it helps me to fall asleep. It does not keep me asleep however, but also does not inhibit dreaming. I personally use it, after consultation with my doctor, to restore a regular sleeping pattern when nothing else works, yet before considering "normal" sleeping pills, because my problem is never insomnia but a circadian rhythm one. I do know that some take it daily, but I would not recommend this without explicit permission and regular follow-up consultations with your doctor. When it comes to this option, always consult your doctor, and maintain a conversation about it whenever there are changes.

The following two "big fixes" also play a major role in a good sleeping pattern, and I would avoid medication before trying these.

Good, nutritious diet

It is an annoying cliché, yet you never escape it. And when you have sensory sensitivities concerning food, it can be extra annoying listening to people telling you to "eat right." But it works.

The fact is that there is no diet that works for everyone. Some people swear by eating gluten-free, but for others it makes no difference at all. I stress this point because most autistic people reap no benefit from limiting their diets in this way. My point is not to tell you to avoid certain things, or to eat a lot of something specific. I am not advocating any particular diet. What I am advocating is a normal, healthy, balanced diet. Everything in moderation, as they say. Try to find ways to make fruits and vegetables appealing to your child. They do not have to like every type of meat, or like meat at all, but it is important to get enough protein, and so on and so forth. Where it is impossible to get them to eat something, for example fish, see if a supplement is available and needed. Again, consult your family doctor. They can take blood tests that show if your child has any vitamin deficiency. You do not have to make your child or household fanatically healthy, just healthy enough. You do not have to cut sugar, carbs, gluten or anything else (unless there are allergies or intolerances involved). Just aim for a regular balanced diet, with regular meals and snacks.

Exercise

Again, a really annoying cliché that actually works. Note that exercise does not necessarily mean running. There are console games that can track movement, in which you can virtually play tennis, bowling, do yoga and many, many other things. Walking is an option. Playing with your dog can be exercise, depending on how you do it. Dancing, swimming, climbing... anything.

But the fact is, regular exercise is good for you. It is not only good for your heart, your other muscles, your blood flow and all that, it is also good for your brain. It releases endorphins, which makes you feel good, and can therefore help manage and reduce depressions. Furthermore, it can also help make you tired for the night, which means your sleep is less likely to be restless and disturbed.

A support system

There will never be a lack of people telling us what we cannot do, what we are bad at and how we are wrong, and there is only one antidote to constantly being told you are wrong, which is also constantly being told you are good, and that you belong.

We, like everybody else, need people around us who appreciate us and who tell us when we do something right. And because we so often make social mistakes which are so often pointed out to us in hurtful ways, we need a little extra awesome in our lives. Immediate family and friends are the source for that awesome. We need you to tell us when we get things right and to give us the, perhaps not physical, high-five when this happens. We need you to be there for us, ready to talk when we finally find the words, patient enough to wait. We need you to listen; we need you to catch us when we fall, and we need you to help us gather the courage to get back up. The importance of a supportive family and friends cannot be overstated. You can mean the difference between a life of depressions and not feeling worthy, and a happy, fulfilling and successful one.

However, sometimes we may need more than a social support system. For those of us who have trouble with comorbid disorders, we can be in need of a financial support system as well. This does not necessarily mean that you support us for our whole lives. What it means is that, for us, knowing that we do not have to worry about surviving can mean the difference between being able to function reasonably and being permanently crippled by the anxiety that if we make a single mistake it will all fall apart. So, depending on who your child is and whether they have extra diagnoses, they may need government support, or they may need to simply know that if it all goes to hell, you will make sure they can eat.

Acceptance

Nothing works without this.

We need you to be okay with our autism. We need you to love us, not in spite of it, but with it. Autism is not "the problem." We do not need to be cured.

What makes life hard for us, in the long run, is not having to compensate for sensory sensitivities, struggling with social skills, impaired executive functions or having really weird interests. What does make life really hard is the people who require that we become like them in order to be accepted. Because we are not like them.

We are not allistic. We are autistic. Our experience and perception of the world is critically different from yours, and that is okay.

If you do not make it into a problem, and instead see our qualities and talents, your whole experience of autism will change, and our whole lives will change. You teach others how to look at us with the way you speak about us and autism, and with the way you react when people say things. Because it can be hard for your child to find the words, you are your child's advocate in this world. You are their voice until they find their own. When we do something not quite "normal" in public and a stranger says something, your response is absorbed in detail. Your response tells the stranger how to see us and it tells onlookers how to see us. It tells them how to see autism.

You also teach us how to look at ourselves. Not to feel wrong, but merely different. Not to feel as though we are worth less than another, but to feel like a human being of equal value. Not to feel ashamed when we are misunderstood, but simply to correct the misunderstanding. To dare to speak at all.

To accept our autism and be okay with who we are, and to feel that we deserve the same respect as anyone else.

This is why the most important thing you will ever teach your child is to accept and appreciate their autism as a part of who they are.

Thank you for reading this book. Thank you for listening to my voice and those of the autistic people who contributed. Thank you for trying to make an autistic person's life better.

References

American Psychiatric Association (2013) *Diagnostic and Statistical Manual of Mental Disorders, Fifth Edition* (DSM-5). Washington, DC: APA.

Attwood, T. (2007) *The Complete Guide to Asperger's Syndrome*. London: Jessica Kingsley Publishers.

Grandin, T. (1984) 'My experiences as an autistic child and review of selected literature.' *Journal of Orthomolecular Psychiatry 13*, 144–174.

Hadcroft, W. (2005) *The Feeling's Unmutual: Growing Up with Asperger Syndrome (Undiagnosed)*. London: Jessica Kingsley Publishers.

Jackson, N. (2002) *Standing Down Falling Up: Asperger's Syndrome from the Inside Out*. Bristol: Lucky Duck Publishing.

Lawson, W. (2001) *Understanding and Working with the Spectrum of Autism: An Insider's View*. London: Jessica Kingsley Publishers.

Milton, D. (2012) 'On the ontological status of autism: the "double empathy problem".' *Disability & Society, 27*, 6, 883–887.

Willey, L.H. (1999) *Pretending to be Normal: Living with Asperger's Syndrome*. London: Jessica Kingsley Publishers.

Williams, D. (1998) *Nobody Nowhere: The Remarkable Autobiography of an Autistic Girl*. London: Jessica Kingsley Publishers.